STUDY GUIDE

FRANCIS X. BRENNAN, PH. D.
Wilkes University

PHYSIOLOGICAL PSYCHOLOGY
A NEUROSCIENCE APPROACH

TIM K. SMOCK

University of Colorado, Boulder

PRENTICE HALL, Upper Saddle River, New Jersey 07458

© 1999 by PRENTICE-HALL, INC.
Simon & Schuster / A Viacom Company
Upper Saddle River, New Jersey 07458

10 9 8 7 6 5 4 3 2 1

Figure 13 : From *The Mind in Sleep* by
Arkin, et al. Reprinted by permission.

Figure 15: Reprinted from NEUROSCIENCE,
Vol. 3, p. 573, figure 2, Amaral and Witter,
The three-dimensional organization of the
hippocampal formation: A review of anatomi-
cal data. Copyright 1989 with permission of
Elsevier Science.

ISBN 0-095802-6

Printed in the United States of America

Table of Contents

Preface

Welcome to the study guide for *PHYSIOLOGICAL PSYCHOLOGY: A NEUROSCIENCE APPROACH*, by Dr. Tim Smock. Tim and I agree that the study of the brain is the most fascinating thing going, and I hope that this guide makes your learning of the material somewhat easier.

Each chapter of the book is covered, and organized the same way. It begins with an overall **summary** of the chapter, emphasizing key points and terms. Next is an **outline** to let you see the total content of each chapter. After the outline is a list of 5-7 **learning objectives**. When you feel you know the chapter well, go back to the learning objectives and treat them like essay questions. If you know the material as well as you think you do, these questions should be no problem. If they pose a problem, it is a good hint to you to go back and review that section of material again.

A **key terms matching exercise** is next. This section will help you identify important terms, definitions, and phrases that appear in the chapter. Next are five **short essay questions** for each chapter. These will overlap somewhat with the learning objectives, but will further test your knowledge of the material in each chapter. Finally, there is a practice test containing **multiple choice questions**. Answers for the matching, essay, and multiple choice questions are provided at the very end of each chapter section.

I hope that this guide makes the study of this fascinating topic easier for you. I welcome any comments or questions you have about the guide. Good luck!

1

Philosophical Issues in Neuroscience

Chapter Summary

This chapter introduces the student to the field of neuroscience, including its history, subdisciplines, and philosophical background. Practical problems to studying the brain are discussed as well as the scientific method. The numerous subdisciplines of neuroscience are listed, as well as the emergence of neuroscience from physiological psychology and neurobiology. The chapter introduces the mind/body problem, and the various historical attempts to answer it. Teleological and deontological reasoning are described, with their relationship to living things and the purpose of life. Developments such as phrenology, and scientists such as Broca and Wernicke, are discussed illustrating the gradual realization that the brain is the seat of consciousness. Finally, the work of Karl Lashley serves to introduce the concepts of **Aggregate Field Theory"** and **Cellular Connectionism**. These two positions differ in their description of the localization of mental function.

Chapter Outline

Studying the Brain

      Practical Concerns:

            Introspection and Received Knowledge

            Scientific Method

The Disciplines of Neuroscience:

    Physiological Psychology and Neurobiology

The Mind/Body Problem:

    Hippocrates and Aristotle

    Descartes

    Box 1-1: Trephining

    Berkeley and La Mettrie

    Do You Have to Choose?

    Box 1-2: Solipsism and Social Relativism

Teleology vs. Deontology:

    Can we Know the Mind of God?

    Does Life Have a Purpose?

    Darwin's Theory

    Teleological Reasoning

The Whole and the Parts:

    Where is the Soul?

    Neurohumors

    The Patients, and Patience, of Paul Broca

    The Law of Equipotentiality

    Box 1-3: Split Brains

    Parallel vs. Serial Processing

Learning Objectives

After completing this chapter, you should be able to:

1. Describe the steps of the scientific method. Also be able to compare and contrast inductive (scientific) vs. deductive (introspection) reasoning.

2. Describe the mind/body problem. List the various "solutions" to it, and what intellectual figures are associated with each.

3. Define "deontology" and "teleology". Explain how evolutionary theory is teleological in nature.

4. Describe the scientific insights associated with Paul Broca and Carl Wernicke.

5. Define the "engram." Discuss Karl Lashley's studies attempting to localize engrams. Explain his conclusions about the physical representation of memory.

6. Describe "aggregate field theory" and "cellular connectionism". Discuss which one is "right" with respect to brain function.

Practice Test

Key Terms-Matching

_____ 1. aggregate field theory   A. associated with absolute dualism

_____ 2. monism   B. processes arise all over the brain at once

_____ 3. deontology   C. things can be explained by their utility

_____ 4. physiological psychology   D. mind and body are identical

_____ 5. La Mettrie   E. study of the biological basis of behavior

_____ 6. interactionist dualism   F. things cannot always be explained by their utility

_____ 7. neuroradiology   G. processes are confined to discrete brain regions

_____ 8. cellular connectionism   H. associated with material monism

_____ 9. Descartes   I. imaging the living brain

_____ 10. teleology   J. mind and body are separate and affect each other

Short Answer Essay Questions

1. What is the mind/body problem? List some of the various "answers" to it along with an intellectual figure associated with each.

2. Briefly describe the work of the American psychologist Karl Lashley attempting to isolate the "engram." What were his conclusions regarding the storage of memories?

3. Compare and contrast aggregate field theory and cellular connectionism. Which one is correct regarding the localization of neural function?

4. How does the scientific method differ from deductive reasoning?

5. Compare and contrast teleological thinking and deontological thinking. With which of these does Darwin's theory of evolution by natural selection fit best?

Multiple Choice Questions

1. A general statement leads to specific conclusions or findings. This describes:
    a. inductive reasoning
    b. a priori truth
    c. deductive reasoning
    d. a posteriori truth

2. Neuroscience emerged as an independent discipline in the 1970s as a combination of:
    a. psychiatry and biology
    b. physiological psychology and neurobiology
    c. psychology and radiology
    d. neuropharmacology and anatomy

3. Given his belief about the mind/body problem, Hippocrates would be considered a/an:
    a. monist
    b. dualist
    c. interactionist dualist
    d. absolute dualist

4. Sir John Eccles used the Heisenberg Uncertainty Principle to attempt to save the notion of:
    a. determinism
    b. a priori truths
    c. emergent properties
    d. free will

5. Solipsism, the belief that you are the only person in the universe, is an extreme form of:
   a. spiritual monism
   b. interactionist dualism
   c. the Heisenberg Uncertainty Principle
   d. materialistic monism

6. Nature, as a creation of the mind of God, is too complex to be understood by the human intellect. This statement epitomizes:
   a. solipsism
   b. teleology
   c. deontology
   d. aggregate field theory

7. A sacred text, considered true without external verification, is an example of:
   a. deductive reasoning
   b. the scientific method
   c. received truth
   d. inductive reasoning

8. Darwin's theory of evolution by natural selection assumes that structures and behaviors all have a purpose. This is an example of:
   a. deontological thinking
   b. teleological thinking
   c. aggregate field theory
   d. monism

9. The pseudoscience of phrenology was associated with:
   a. Gall
   b. Broca
   c. Darwin
   d. Wernicke

10. In the parlance of cognitive neuroscience, serial processing is synonymous with:
    a. monism
    b. parallel processing
    c. cellular connectionism
    d. aggregate field theory

11. Specific observations lead to general truths. This describes:
    a. deductive reasoning
    b. introspection
    c. inductive reasoning
    d. heuristic imagery

12.   Broca's patients all exhibited aphasia. This is the inability to:
    a. learn
    b. smell
    c. communicate
    d. remember events

13.   According to Lashley, the physical basis of a memory was called the:
    a. engram
    b. law of equipotentiality
    c. temporal lobe
    d. decussation

14.   Which of the following terms is out of place?
    a. observation
    b. introspection
    c. experiment
    d. conclusion

15.   Aristotle's position on the mind/body problem put him in agreement with:
    a. La Mettrie
    b. Hippocrates
    c. Berkeley
    d. Descartes

Labeling Exercise

1.   Please label this diagram using the terms listed.

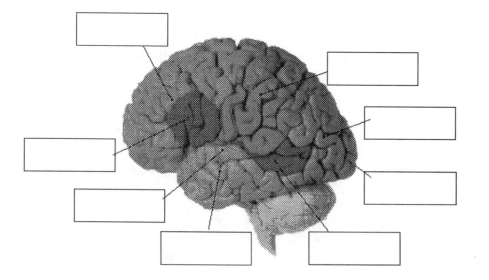

Broca's Area

Frontal Lobe

Occipital Lobe

Parietal Lobe

Primary Auditory Area

Primary Visual Area

Temporal Lobe

Wernicke's Area

Answers

Key-Terms Matching

1.	B	6.	J
2.	D	7.	I
3.	F	8.	G
4.	E	9.	A
5.	H	10.	C

Short Answer Essay Questions

1. The mind/body problem is an ancient philosophical debate concerning the relationship between the physical and spiritual realms. In neuroscience, it takes the form of whether or not the mind and body are the same or different. If they are indeed different, how do they interact, if at all? Hippocrates, after treating patients with brain injuries, concluded that mind and body are identical, a position called monism. Aristotle disagreed, asserting that there is a nonphysical realm separate from the brain or body. This position is called dualism. Descartes further refined dualistic thinking by arguing that mind and body can influence each other. This brand of dualism is labeled interactionist dualism. Two other famous historical figures are associated with the only two logical kinds of monism. Bishop George Berkeley asserted that the material world was illusory, and everything was nonphysical or spiritual. La Mettrie, a French philosopher, argued that all reality was in fact physical, denying the existence of any nonphysical realm.

2. Lashley, as a good monist, assumed that memory formation would produce a physical change in the brain. He further assumed that the engram, or physical change itself, would be stored in one location of the cortex. Therefore, he taught rats to solve a maze to receive a food reward. He then lesioned parts of the cortex and examined the effect on the animals memory of the maze. Removing any small part of the cortex produced no change in maze running behavior. Only when large sections of cortex were removed was there a drop in performance. Lashley concluded that memories were not stored in one spot, but rather were spread diffusely throughout the cortex. He called this idea the "law of equipotentiality."

3. Aggregate field theory describes processes that appear to arise everywhere at once, or at least to be evenly distributed across various brain regions. In the lingo of cognitive neuroscience, this view would be called parallel processing. Cellular connectionism is conceptually the opposite, describing functions that appear to be highly localized to certain brain regions. There are data to support both positions. Lashley's work with brain lesions and maze memory appears to support aggregate field theory, while the works of Broca and Wernicke appears to be best interpreted by cellular connectionism.

4. Deductive reasoning in general is the application of general truths to specific statements. General truths are derived from introspection or religious doctrine, and specific statements are deduced from them. The primary problem is lack of agreement on the general truths that we start with. The scientific method, as an example of inductive reasoning, proceeds in the opposite direction. Specific observations lead to general truths. More specifically, specific observations lead to hypotheses about observed regularities, which lead to experiments to test those hypotheses, which lead to conclusions about the acceptance or rejection of the hypotheses.

5. Deontological thinking assumes that the purpose of things in nature cannot be ascertained, because the mind of God which created those things is too complex. The mind of humans is too feeble to understand the utility of things, if indeed a utility exists at all. Teleological thinking, on the other hand, assumes that nature would reflect the perfectly rational mind of God. Humans, although significantly less powerful than God, could still attempt to glean order and purpose from nature. Darwin's theory of evolution by natural selection, although not classically religious in nature, adopted much of teleological thinking. Darwinian thinking assumed that every structure or behavior must have a purpose or function, or natural selection would not have selected for it.

Multiple Choice Answers

1. C
2. B
3. A
4. D
5. A
6. C
7. C
8. B

9. A
10. D
11. C
12. C
13. A
14. B
15. D

The Cellular Basis of Behavior

Chapter Summary

This chapter introduces the student to the "star" of the show, the neuron. Neurons are specialized cells to transmit information within the nervous system. That fact wasn't fully realized until the twentieth century. Some scientists, like Camillo Golgi, believed in **Reticular Theory**, the idea that the brain was a continuous network of fibers. The belief that the brain was cellular, like all other tissue, became known as the **Neuron Doctrine**. That position was associated with the neuroscientist Ramon y Cajal, who ironically came to his conclusions by staining brain tissue with a stain invented by Golgi! The parts of neurons are discussed, as well as the "law of dynamic polarization," the notion that information flow within a neuron proceeds from dendrite to soma to axon. The special properties and structure of the plasma membrane are discussed. The chapter also introduces the student to basic genetics. Genetic information exists on strands of DNA, arranged in a double helix shape. The formation of a strand of messenger RNA (mRNA) is a process called *transcription*. At the ribosomes, the mRNA is *translated* into protein. Proteins perform a myriad of functions relevant for neuroscience, including acting as receptors, hormones, enzymes, and their functions. Transport of materials within a neuron, as well as endo- and ectocytosis are discussed. Finally, the development of neurons and the formation of synapses are discussed. Classic research by Roger Sperry is discussed that appears to indicate that during development neurons are attracted by chemicals that guide them to their appropriate targets.

Chapter Outline

Neuron Doctrine vs. Reticular Theory:

    Is the Brain Cells, or a Web?

Learning Objectives

After completing this chapter, you should be able to:

1. Differentiate between "Reticular Theory" and the "Neuron Doctrine". List which famous neuroscientist is associated with each position, and describe what is now views as the correct answer.

2. Describe the basic structure of the plasma membrane. Describe why the membrane looks the way it does using the concepts of hydrophilicity and hydrophobicity.

3. Detail the formation of protein from DNA to RNA to ribosome.

4. List some of the functions that proteins perform in the nervous system.

5. Describe orthograde and retrograde transport, exocytosis and endocytosis.

6. Elucidate the chemoaffinity hypothesis. Describe Roger Sperry's famous experiment supporting it.

7. Describe glycolysis, aerobic metabolism, and proton transfer.

Practice Test

Key Terms-Matching

____ 1. Neuron Doctrine   A. hydrophobic

____ 2. "water loving"   B. monopolar cell

____ 3. away from the soma   C. hydrophilic

____ 4. adenine   D. protein synthesis

____ 5. single neurite   E. Cajal

____ 6. ribosomes   F. retrograde transport

____ 7. "water fearing"   G. cytosine

____ 8. toward the soma   H. Golgi

____ 9. Reticular Theory   I. thymine

____ 10. guanine   J. anterograde transport

Short Answer Essay Questions

1. Compare and contrast Reticular Theory and the Neuron Doctrine.

2. Briefly summarize the formation of protein from the chromosome to the ribosome.

3. Describe Sperry's famous experiment with salamander eyes. What did the results imply about how the brain develops?

4. Describe some of the functions that proteins perform relevant for neuroscience.

5. What is the "Law of Dynamic Polarization?" Is it correct?

Multiple Choice Questions

1. Translation occurs in the:
    a. Golgi bodies
    b. ribosomes
    c. lysosomes
    d. nucleus

2. The release of the contents of a vesicle into the extracellular fluid describes:
    a. exocytosis
    b. endocytosis
    c. clathrinization
    d. axoplasmic transport

3. In the Perpiheral Nervous System (PNS), myelin is provided by:
    a. oligodendrocytes
    b. astrocytes
    c. neurites
    d. Schwann cells

4. A devoted disciple of reticular theory was:
    a. Cajal
    b. Sperry
    c. Golgi
    d. Levi-Montalcini

5. Boutons exist:
    a. throughout the cell
    b. at the end of axons
    c. in every dendrite
    d. at the junction of the soma and axon

6. The "Law of Dynamic Polarization" as articulated by Cajal says that information proceeds from:
   a. axon to cell body to dendrite
   b. cell body to dendrite to axon
   c. cell body to axon to cell body
   d. dendrite to cell body to axon

7. The process of transcription produces a single strand of:
   a. tRNA
   b. DNA
   c. protein
   d. mRNA

8. Proteins that span the cell membrane *must be*:
   a. amphipathic
   b. hydrophobic
   c. hydrophilic
   d. promoters

9. The energy produced by glycolysis is in the form of:
   a. pyruvate
   b. NADH
   c. ATP
   d. citric acid

10. The movement of materials away from the soma describes:
    a. retrograde transport
    b. anterograde transport
    c. neurofilamentation
    d. phosphorylation

11. The tip of a growing axon is called a:
    a. microspike
    b. growth cone
    c. trophic factor
    d. postsynaptic density

12. Roger Sperry's famous experiments rotating salamander eyes generated empirical support for the:
    a. Neuron Doctrine
    b. Reticular Theory
    c. Law of Dynamic Polarization
    d. Chemoaffinity Hypothesis

13. Adenine is to thymine as guanine is to:
    a. cytosine
    b. ATP
    c. valine
    d. sofa

14. Another name for aerobic metabolism is:
    a. glycolysis
    b. pyruvate transfer
    c. Krebs cycle
    d. proton transfer

15. The Neuron Doctrine is associated with:
    a. Cajal
    b. Golgi
    c. Sperry
    d. Descartes

Labeling Exercises

1. Please label the letters in this diagram using the terms listed.

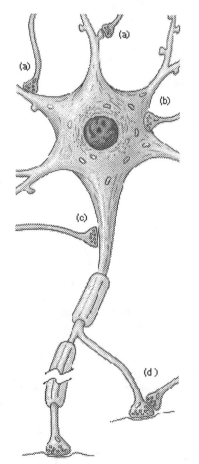

A contact on the soma (axosomatic contact)

A synapse onto another axon (axoaxonic contact)

A synapse where a bouton can both send and receive a signal (axosynaptic contact)

A Synapse onto a dendrite (axodendritic contact)

2. Please label this diagram using the terms listed.

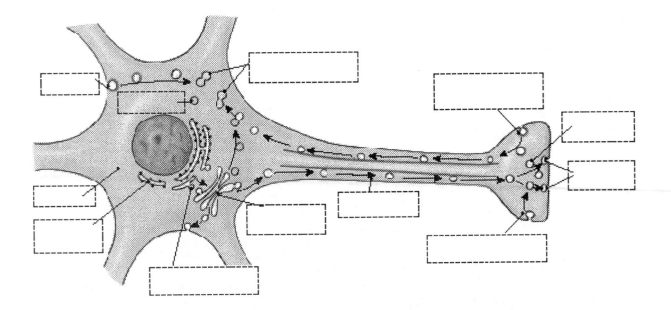

Axon
Constitutive endocytosis
Endocytosis in nerve terminal and transport to the soma
Exocytosis
Golgi apparatus
Lysosome
Lysosome degradation of endocytic vesicles
Membrane synthesis in the soma
Rough endoplasmic reticulum
Soma
Synaptic vesicle
Synaptic vesicle recycling in nerve terminal

Answers

Key Terms Matching

1.	E	6.	D
2.	C	7.	A
3.	J	8.	F
4.	I	9.	H
5.	B	10.	G

Short Answer Essay Questions

1. Reticular Theory, associated with Golgi, was the position that the brain was a continuous web of fibers, and not composed of individual cells. The Neuron Doctrine, associated with Cajal, was the belief that the brain was similar to the rest of the body and was composed of specialized cells called neurons. Cajal, ironically using a stain named for Golgi, was able to stain brain tissue and ascertain that the brain in fact was composed of individual cells. Although still unable to visualize synapses, Cajal came to his conclusion after observing that various parts of the tissue would stain (the perikarya) and other regions would not. This finding, he believed, was incompatible with the notion of the brain as a continuous web of tissue.

2. Protein synthesis begins in the chromosomes along segments of DNA. An enzyme, RNA polymerase, interacts with segments of DNA (genes) and makes an RNA copy of it. This process is called transcription, and involves the construction of messenger RNA (mRNA). The mRNA is constructed by matching complementary base pairs along the DNA sequence. The completed mRNA leaves the nucleus and travels to the ribosomes where the process of translation begins. Translation is the reading of the mRNA by a second kind of RNA, transfer RNA (tRNA). The tRNA carries with it one of twenty amino acids that are assembled into protein. The number, kind, and place of each amino acid determines which of the many thousands of different proteins is constructed.

3. Nobel-Prize winning neuroscientist Roger Sperry conducted studies to determine how developing axons and neurons find their way to their appropriate targets. He used the eyes of salamanders for his experiments. Salamanders were chosen because they, like other amphibians, are capable of regeneration of axons if they are severed. In the most famous study, he severed the axons leaving the back of the salamander eye heading for the tectum. He then rotated the eyes one hundred and eighty degrees and reinserted them. The possibilities were endless. If the axons were merely following some preprogrammed pattern, then they would continue to grow and reattach to the wrong targets. However, if the axons were being attracted to the target by some chemical, then they should reattach to the original targets, even though they would now be in a different location. In fact, the axons reattached to their original targets, supporting the idea that chemicals called trophic factors guide neurons to their targets during development. This idea has received other empirical support and has been named the Chemoaffinity Hypothesis.

4. Proteins perform a myriad of functions relevant for brain functioning. Some proteins, such as actin and tubulin, have a structural role in supporting the shape of the cell, as well as transport of materials within a cell. Other protein molecules function as enzymes, which drive chemical reactions. Finally, some amphipathic protein molecules form receptors which span the cell membrane, and are the site of neurotransmitter action. Some receptors are complex molecules that form channels for specific ions to pass through.

5. The Law of Dynamic Polarization is attributed to Ramon y Cajal. He argued that information flow in the nervous system is unidirectional. He surmised this function, given the structure of most neurons. Given the fact that there are many dendrites and one axon in most neurons, the dendrites seem like information gathering regions of the cell, and the axon seems ideal for the integration and output of that information. The Law, therefore, was that information flow proceeds from dendrite to soma to axon, then across the synapse to the dendrite of another neuron. The "Law" is generally correct given the many axodendritic synapses that are observed. However, observation also reveals axons connecting with cell bodies (axosomatic contacts) and other axons directly (axoaxonic contacts). Finally, a bouton can also receive a contact from another axon (axosynaptic contact). Therefore, the law of dynamic polarization, as formulated by Cajal, does not appear to be completely correct.

Multiple Choice Answers

1.	B	9.	C
2.	A	10.	B
3.	D	11.	B
4.	C	12.	D
5.	B	13.	A
6.	D	14.	C
7.	D	15.	A
8.	A		

3

Communication among Neurons: Membrane Potentials

Chapter Summary

This chapter introduces the student to the concept of membrane potentials. To fully understand this concept requires the introduction of some basic ideas from chemistry. Molecules are comprised of atoms, which are elementary particles composed of a nucleus and orbiting electrons. Atoms or molecules that have either lost or gained electrons have an electrical charge, and are called ions. Like charges repel, and opposite charges attract. This fact is referred to as **Enthalpy.** This rule, along with the fact that molecules diffuse from areas of greater to lesser concentrations, called **Entropy,** contributes to the state of the neuron at rest. Ions "wish" to travel across the cell membrane to either move down their concentration gradient, or because of attraction from an opposite charge. The membrane is not permeable to ions, however, and they can only pass through specific doors or channels. Each ion species can be described as at equilibrium when the forces of entropy and enthalpy are precisely balanced. The formula for calculating the equilibrium potential for the three major ions (potassium, sodium, and chloride) is the **Nernst Equation**. The formula for calculating the potential of the entire membrane is the **Goldman Equation**. The Goldman Equation comes very close to the actual value of the membrane potential, which can be experimentally measured. The small discrepancy comes from the **Sodium/Potassium Pump**, an enzyme that moves sodium out of the cell and potassium into the cell. The equilibrium potentials of the three major ion species can be considered batteries. The channels or gates that the ions travel through can be seen as conductors. We can describe these electrical processes using **Ohm's Law**. An important fact to remember is that the equilibrium potentials, or batteries, never change. The conductances change, and that fact leads to the action potential and all of the other higher processes to be discussed later.

Chapter Outline

The Basics of Chemistry

    How Matter Behaves:

        Opposite Charges Attract

        Quantity and Concentration

A Semipermeable Membrane

    The Inside and the Outside Differ:

        Entropy and Enthalpy

        An "Equilibrium Potential" for Potassium

        Box 3-1: The Nernst Equation and the Goldman Equation

Measuring the Membrane Potential

    What is the Value of the Difference?

    Polarity and Ground

    Depolarization and Hyperpolarization

Three Forces and Three Gates

    "The Batteries do not Change!"

    Nernst Values for Sodium and Chloride

    Permeability Ratios

    The Goldman Equation

    The Sodium/Potassium Pump

The "Equivalent Circuit"

    Chemicals That Carry a Charge:

        Batteries and Conductors

        Box 3-2: Ohm's Law Simplified

        Constancy of the Batteries

        Variability of the Conductances

        Box 3-3: A Biologist's Definition of Life and Death

Learning Objectives

After completing this chapter, you should be able to:

1. Describe the forces of entropy and enthalpy, and how they are relevant for the resting membrane potential.

2. Mathematically produce the equilibrium potential for any ion species using the Nernst Equation.

3. Calculate the predicted value of the membrane potential using the Goldman Equation.

4. Describe Ohm's Law, its relevance to membrane processes, and conductance.

5. Describe the "equivalent circuit."

6. Describe how we can measure the actual membrane potential.

Practice Test

Key Terms-Matching

_____ 1. mhos	A.	units of resistance
_____ 2. entropy	B.	like charges repel
_____ 3. anions	C.	diffusion as an example
_____ 4. -93 mV	D.	E_{Na}
_____ 5. -70 mV	E.	units of conductance
_____ 6. ohms	F.	E_{Cl}
_____ 7. -66 mV	G.	particles with a positive charge
_____ 8. +56 mV	H.	V_M
_____ 9. cations	I.	E_k
_____ 10. enthalpy	J.	particles with a negative charge

Short Answer Essay Questions

1. Describe the forces of entropy and enthalpy.

2. Why is V_M slightly different from the predicted value ($E_{M)}$ using the Goldman Equation?

3. What is an "equilibrium potential?"

4. What is Ohm's Law? What is resistance? What is conductance?

5. Describe the concept of the "equivalent circuit."

Multiple Choice Questions

1. Atoms bond together with other atoms to form:
    a. elements
    b. protons
    c. molecules
    d. complexes

2. Potassium ions will tend to be pushed out of cells by:
    a. entropy
    b. enthalpy
    c. electrostatic pressure
    d. a & b

3. Anything that increases the charge difference between the inside and the outside of cells represents a:
    a. depolarization
    b. hypopolarization
    c. hyperpolarization
    d. EPSP

4. The ion species that has the highest permeability ratio at rest is:
    a. chloride
    b. potassium
    c. sodium
    d. calcium

5. One can calculate the "equilibrium potential" for an ion species using the:
    a. Nernst Equation
    b. Goldman Equation
    c. permeability ratios
    d. electrometer

6. [K]O represents the:
   a. concentration of sodium outside the cell
   b. concentration of potassium inside the cell
   c. concentration of potassium outside the cell
   d. permeability ratio for potassium

7. Using the Goldman equation, Hodgkin, Huxley, and Katz arrived at a value of _____ for E_m.
   a. -67 mV
   b. -70 mV
   c. +56 mV
   d. +67 mV

8. The difference between the predicted value of the membrane potential using the Goldman equation, and the *actual* value is due to:
   a. measurement error
   b. the Goldman Equation ignoring Ca++
   c. resistance
   d. the sodium/potassium pump

9. The inverse of resistance is:
   a. conductance
   b. voltage
   c. current
   d. potential

10. Which of the following can change?
    a. E_K
    b. E_{Cl}
    c. E_{Na}
    d. none of the above

11. A cathode:
    a. attracts cations
    b. attracts anions
    c. repels anions
    d. attracts negative charge

12. V is to potential as I is to:
    a. conductance
    b. current
    c. ohms
    d. resistance

13. The fact that sugar will diffuse and become more or less evenly distributed throughout a cup of coffee demonstrates:
    a. electrostatic pressure
    b. enthalpy
    c. entropy
    d. none of the above

14. -93 mV is the:
    a. resting membrane potential
    b. equilibrium potential for sodium
    c. equilibrium potential for chloride
    d. equilibrium potential for potassium

15. Aside from including all three major ion species, the important force covered in the Goldman Equation but not the Nernst Equation is:
    a. permeability
    b. inside concentration
    c. outside concentration
    d. the ideal gas constant

Labeling Exercises

1. Please complete this table using the terms listed.

Table 3-2	CONCENTRATION IN mM		
Ion	Intracellular	Extracellular (Sea Water)	Blood
	400	10	20
	50	460	440
	40	540	560
	0.1	10	10

calcuim (Ca^+)

chloride (Cl^+)

potassium (K^+)

sodium (Na^+)

2. Please label this diagram using the terms listed.

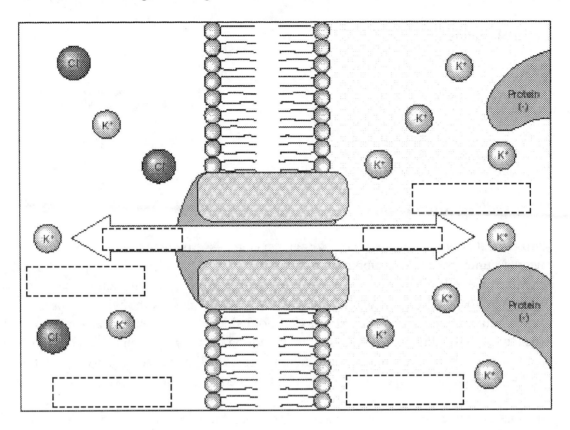

Electrostatic
Entropy
High potassium concentration
Inside becomes cathode (-)
Low potassium concentration
Outside becomes anode (+)

Answers

Key Terms Matching

1.	E		6.	A
2.	C		7.	F
3.	J		8.	D
4.	I		9.	G
5.	H		10.	B

Short Answer Essay Questions

1. Entropy is the force in nature that makes any system less organized. For the cell membrane, unequal numbers of a given ion species on either side of the membrane represents order or organization. Therefore, the force of entropy will tend to drive ions across the membrane, down their concentration gradients, to make both sides equal. Although perhaps counterintuitive, equal amounts of an ion species on both sides of a cell membrane represents less order than unequal amounts. Enthalpy is the notion that opposite charges attract and same charges repel. For the cell membrane, an ion species will be attracted across the membrane if it has an opposite charge and repelled if it has the same charge.

2. One can empirically measure the value of the membrane potential using microelectrodes. Doing this, the value of the charge difference between the inside and the outside of the cell (V_M) is approximately -70 mV. One can mathematically calculate the value of the membrane potential using the Goldman equation. The Goldman equation is essentially a big Nernst Equation, calculating and combining equilibrium potentials for each of the three major ion species. The Goldman equation also uses permeability ratios, however, which factor in how much each ion species can actually affect the membrane potential. Using the Goldman equation, the predicted value of the membrane potential (E_M) is -67 mV. Although very close, the Goldman equation clearly delivers the incorrect answer. The reason for the small discrepancy is an enzyme known as the sodium/potassium pump. The pump pushes any sodium ions that have leaked into the cell back out, and pulls back any potassium ions that have exited the cell. Curiously, for most nerve cells it is not an even 1:1 transfer of sodium to potassium. Rather, for every three sodium ions removed from the cell, only two potassium ions are pulled back in. The pump is therefore electrogenic, meaning it creates a current. It is the reason that the actual membrane potential (V_M) is slightly more negative than the predicted value (E_M).

3. An "equilibrium potential" for a given ion species represents a balance between the forces of entropy and enthalpy. At some point, the force of diffusion pushing ions in or out of the cell will be exactly balanced by electrostatic pressure. The amount of electrostatic pressure can be represented by an electrical potential in millivolts. The equilibrium potentials for the major ion species can be calculated using the Nernst equation. Another way to think of it,

somewhat anthropomorphically, is that the value of the equilibrium potential for each ion species is the value that each ion "wants" the membrane potential to be.

4. Ohm's Law is a description of relationships between potentials, current, and resistance for electrical processes. The mathematical formula for Ohm's law is $V=IR$. V stands for the potential in volts, I is the current in amps, and R is the resistance in ohms. Basically, Ohm's Law shows that current is high when resistance is low, and current is low when resistance is high. Resistance blocks the flow of current. This is symbolized by the floodgates being closed like in the analogy presented in Box 3-2. Conductance is the reciprocal of resistance, and is more commonly used when discussing biological systems.

5. The "equivalent circuit" is a model of the membrane potential describing events in electrical terms. This model allows one to focus exclusively on batteries and conductors. Looking at things this way enables one to dispense with gradients and forces. Each of the three equilibrium potentials for the three major ion species can be considered batteries in a literal sense. These never change. The conductors, in terms of the membrane, would be the gates that permit the ions to flow in and out of the cell. The conductances do change. This electrical model of the membrane subsumes the description of ions, gradients, and forces.

Multiple Choice Answers

1.	C	9.	A
2.	A	10.	D
3.	C	11.	A
4.	B	12.	B
5.	A	13.	C
6.	C	14.	D
7.	A	15.	A
8.	D		

4

Communication Among Neurons:
The Action Potential

Chapter Summary

This chapter introduces the student to the concept of action potentials. Neurons are divided into chemically excitable regions and electrically excitable regions. The chemically excitable region consists of the soma and dendrites, and is the subject of the next chapter. The electrically excitable region consists of the axon and boutons. Brief depolarizations called **Action Potentials** are the basis of neural signaling in the electrically excitable domain. All action potentials are identical, a phenomenon called the **All-or-None Law**. If a neuron reaches a particular voltage known as its **threshold,** an action potential will occur. The neuron exhibits a transient state of inexcitability after an action potential called **refractoriness.** The action potential is produced by a combination of sodium and potassium currents. At threshold, sodium conductance increases, enabling a depolarizing sodium current to enter the cell. The sodium current is only active for approximately one millisecond, and is thus both **voltage-dependent** and **time-dependent**. As the sodium conductance decreases, the conductance for potassium increases, causing a hyperpolarizing current which returns the cell to its resting potential. Both the sodium and potassium channels are selective, sensitive to voltage, and have timing mechanisms. Most channel types come in different versions, a concept called **heterogeneity**. Many exhibit regions of similarity, however a concept called **homology** appears to indicate a common evolutionary ancestor. Transmission of an action potential down a myelinated axon is referred to as **saltatory conduction**. Finally, at the bouton, there are channels for calcium. Calcium entering the neuron causes the exocytosis of neurotransmitter molecules into the synaptic cleft, the subject of the next chapter.

Chapter Outline

The Electrically Excitable Domain

    Axons and Boutons:

        An All-or-None Event

        Threshold and Refractoriness

        Box 4-1: The Giant Squid Axon and the Voltage Clamp

        The Real Basis of the Action Potential

The Action Potential Explained

    Sodium and Potassium:

        Two Currents Drive the Action Potential

        The Effects of Toxins on Current

        How Conductances Create the Waveform

Functions of the Sodium Channel

    The Sodium Channel as a Selectivity Filter

    The Sodium Channel as a Voltage Sensor

    The Sodium Channel as a Time Sensor

    The Sodium Channel as an Inactivation Mechanism

Functions of the Potassium Channel

    The Potassium Channel as a Selectivity Filter

    The Potassium Channel as a Voltage Sensor

    The Potassium Channel as a Delay Mechanism

Learning Objectives

After completing this chapter, you should be able to:

1. Describe the "chemically excitable" and "electrically excitable" domains of the neuron.

2. Elucidate the two major currents that produce the observed action potential.

3. Describe heterogeneity and homology in regard to channels, receptors, etc.

4. Describe saltatory conduction.

5. Discuss the "voltage clamp" procedure and how it enabled neuroscientists to discover the ionic mechanisms of the action potential.

6. Describe the role of calcium in neurotransmitter release.

Practice Test

Key-Terms Matching

_____ 1. axons and boutons

_____ 2. saltatory conduction

_____ 3. refractoriness

_____ 4. sodium

_____ 5. TTX

_____ 6. postsynaptic

_____ 7. potassium

_____ 8. TEA

_____ 9. dendrites and soma

_____ 10. presynaptic

A. blocks the sodium channel

B. "falling phase" of the action potential

C. action potential traveling down a myelinated axon

D. "before the synapse"

E. "chemically excitable domain"

F. "rising phase" of the action potential

G. "electrically excitable domain"

H. "state of inexcitability"

I. "after the synapse"

J. blocks the potassium channel

Short Answer Essay Questions

1. What is the difference between the electrically excitable and chemically excitable regions of a neuron?

2. What are the two major currents that produce the action potential?

3. What are some properties of sodium and potassium channels that are relevant for the action potential?

4. What is saltatory conduction? Why is it faster than non-saltatory conduction?

5. What is the role of calcium in the action potential and the release of transmitter?

Multiple Choice Questions

1. The "electrically excitable domain" is comprised of the:
   a. axon
   b. soma
   c. dendrites
   d. all of the above

2. The peak of the action potential approaches:
   a. E_{Cl}
   b. E_K
   c. G_{Cl}
   d. E_{Na}

3. The value of a stimulus that just barely causes an action potential is the:
   a. depolarization
   b. hyperpolarization
   c. threshold
   d. refractory period

4. Tetrodotoxin (TTX) appears to:
   a. block the potassium channel
   b. block the sodium channel
   c. activate the calcium channel
   d. change G_{Cl}

5. Since sodium conductance changes at a particular value (threshold), we say the it is:
   a. time dependent
   b. time independent
   c. voltage dependent
   d. invariable

6. As sodium conductance falls during an action potential:
   a. potassium conductance increases
   b. potassium conductance falls
   c. calcium conductance rises
   d. chloride conductance falls

7. The sodium channel is composed of _____ monomers.
   a. 1
   b. 4
   c. 3
   d. 11

8. Tetraethylammonium (TEA) appears to:
    a. block the potassium channel
    b. block the sodium channel
    c. activate the calcium channel
    d. change G_{Cl}

9. The fact that different channels, which are coded for by different genes, are often very structurally similar is referred to as:
    a. heterogeneity
    b. homogeneity
    c. heterology
    d. homology

10. The conduction of an action potential down a myelinated axon is called:
    a. Mauthner conduction
    b. heterogeneous conduction
    c. saltatory conduction
    d. refractoriness

11. The ion species that has channels located only in the bouton is:
    a. sodium
    b. calcium
    c. potassium
    d. chloride

12. The "voltage clamp" technique enables researchers to:
    a. eliminate all voltage from an axon
    b. modify Ohm's Law
    c. eliminate sodium from the neuron
    d. maintain voltage in a system at any value desired by the experimenter

13. Much of the pioneering research in neurophysiology was conducted with the giant axon of the:
    a. squid
    b. monkey
    c. dolphin
    d. buffalo

14. During an action potential, the sodium gate remains open for approximately:
    a. 1 millisecond
    b. 10 milliseconds
    c. 100 milliseconds
    d. 1 second

15. Conduction of an action potential from one end of the axon to the bouton refers to:
    a. antidromic flow
    b. orthograde transmission
    c. orthodromic flow
    d. anterograde flow

Labeling Exercises

1. Please label this diagram using these terms: Na+   K+   Cl-

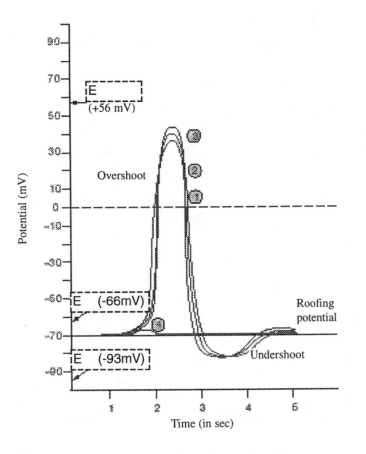

2.   Please label this diagram using these terms: V_M g^{Na} g_K

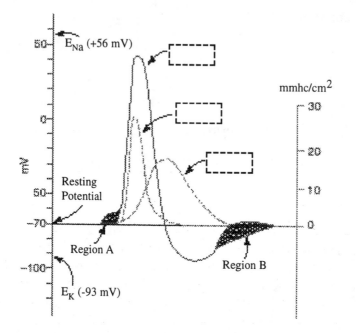

Answers

Key Terms Matching

1. G
2. C
3. H
4. F
5. A

6. I
7. B
8. J
9. E
10. D

Short Answer Essay Questions

1. Neurons are divided into an electrically excitable region, comprised of axons and boutons, and a chemically excitable region, comprised of dendrites and somas. These two regions, or domains, of neurons differ in the forces that cause the gates to open and close. The dendrites and soma are sensitive to the presence of neurotransmitter molecules from other cells, and are thus designed to receive signals. The axons and boutons are sensitive to small electrical changes at the axon hillock, and transmit these changes down the boutons. They, therefore, are designed to transmit information across the synapse to the chemically excitable domain of other neurons.

2. The brief depolarization known as the action potential is the basis of signaling in the electrically excitable domain of neurons. Action potentials are cause by two currents: one for sodium, and one for potassium. At the threshold of excitation, sodium conductance increases, causing an influx of sodium into the cell. This sodium current causes the cell to pass zero, and approach the equilibrium potential for sodium, although it does not reach it. The channels for sodium are time-dependent, meaning that they are only open for a brief period of time, approximately one millisecond. As the sodium conductance is declining, the conductance for potassium is increasing. This causes a potassium current, produced by potassium ions leaving the cell. This is a hyperpolarizing current, and essentially returns the cell to the resting membrane potential. The action potential can be viewed as the action of the sodium current depolarizing the membrane, followed by the potassium current returning the membrane to normal.

3. The two channels, one specific for sodium and one specific for potassium, have a number of characteristics relevant for the action potential. The sodium channel, first, is selective for sodium ions. The actual basis of channel selectivity is still receiving much research attention. The channel for sodium also is a voltage sensor, able to detect the membrane potential. When the membrane reaches the threshold point, a strip inside the channel physically moves and allows sodium ions to enter the cell. The sodium channel also functions as a timer, leaving the channel open for only a brief period of time before closing. Finally, the channel also appears to be connected to an "inactivation gate", making the cell refractory until the gate is removed. The potassium channel also functions as a selectivity filter and a

voltage sensor, as the sodium channel does. The potassium channel also functions as a delay mechanism, delaying the opening of the potassium gate for a millisecond. This delay coincides with the length of time the sodium channel is open and allows sodium to depolarize the cell.

4. Saltatory conduction is the transmission of an action potential down a myelinated axon. The term comes from the Latin word "to leap". In a myelinated axon, the equivalent circuit becomes larger and current only travels though the nodes of Ranvier. When the inward current predominates at a particular node, the current must travel all the way to the next node before the outward current can escape. Therefore, the action potential "leaps" from node to node down the axon. In a nonmyelinated cell, the equivalent circuit travels down each small region of membrane, and is thus significantly slower.

5. Calcium, a divalent action, becomes relevant to the action potential at the bouton. There are voltage-dependent calcium channels that exist only at the bouton. In response to an action potential, calcium enters the cell through these channels. Calcium binds to both synaptic vesicles that contain the neurotransmitter molecules, and to the inside of the plasma membrane. Enzymes such as calmodulin assist in the process of the vesicle fusing with the membrane exocytotically. The site of vesicular fusion is referred to as the "active zone". This cause the neurotransmitter substance to be dumped into the synaptic cleft.

Multiple Choice Answers

1.	A	9.	D
2.	D	10.	C
3.	C	11.	B
4.	B	12.	D
5.	C	13.	A
6.	A	14.	A
7.	B	15.	C
8.	A		

Communications Among Neurons: Synaptic Potentials

Chapter Summary

This chapter introduces the student to the concept of synaptic potentials. The chemically excitable domain, comprised of the dendrites and soma of the cell, does not experience all-or-none action potentials as the electrically excitable domain does. Rather, it experiences **postsynaptic potentials** that are temporally longer and also incremental. Synaptic potentials that are conducive to action potential generation are called **EPSP's**, and those that tend to prevent action potentials are called **IPSP's**. Dendrites typically receive many inputs. The reduction of all of these inputs into action potentials is called **integration**. EPSP's and IPSP's can summate over both space (**spatial summation**), and time (**temporal summation**). Synaptic transmission is said to be **quantal** in nature, that is incremental. Neurotransmitter molecules do not enter the postsynaptic cell, but rather interact with specific protein molecules embedded in the membrane called **receptors**. **Agonists** bind to receptors and activate them, whereas **antagonists** bind to receptors and do not activate them. Allosteric modifiers bind to a location different from the binding site of agonists and antagonists. The best understood transmitter molecule is **acetylcholine**, the substance at the **neuromuscular junction** that also exists in brain. The major inhibitory transmitter in brain appears to be Gamma-aminobutyric acid (**GABA**). Other transmitter substances include glutamate, aspartate, glycine, and the catecholamines, dopamine and norepinephrine. Larger molecules like **peptides** also function as neurotransmitter molecules in the brain. Some substances in the brain seem to act as neuromodulators, their only activity being to influence the action of other neurotransmitters. Finally, electrotonic synapses have been identified, which do not use transmitters, but rather are a direct electrical connection between cells.

Chapter 5   Communications Among Neurons: Synaptic Potentials

Chapter Outline

Learning Objectives

After completing this chapter, you should be able to:

1. Describe EPSP's and IPSP's, summation and integration.

2. Discuss the "quantal nature" of synaptic transmission, including the theories of quantal transmission.

3. Describe Otto Loewi's famous experiment that demonstrated conclusively that transmission at synapses is a chemical event.

4. Discuss the synthesis and breakdown of acetylcholine, and its role at the neuromuscular junction.

5. Describe the importance of GABA in brain.

6. List the classic criteria for identifying neurotransmitter molecules in brain.

7. Discuss the concept of neuropeptides and neuromodulation.

Practice Test

Key-Terms Matching

____ 1. "Vagusstoff"   A. substance produced by the body

____ 2. antagonist   B. block receptors

____ 3. EPSP   C. neuromuscular junction

____ 4. nicotine   D. allosteric to GABA

____ 5. exogenous   E. activate receptors

____ 6. end plates   F. conducive to action potentials

____ 7. agonist   G. foreign substances

____ 8. endogenous   H. acetylcholine

____ 9. barbiturate   I. cholinergic agonist

____ 10. IPSP   J. prevent action potentials

Short Answer Essay Questions

1. What are summation and integration? How do they function to excite or inhibit the cell?

2. What are the two types of ligands possible for receptors?

3. Describe some of the drugs that affect cholinergic synapses.

4. What is neuromodulation? How has the concept of neurotransmission become more complex in recent years?

5. What is an electrotonic synapse? What kinds of behaviors appear to be mediated by these synapses?

Multiple Choice Questions

1. Synaptic potentials that are conducive to action potential generation are:
   a. IPSPs
   b. EPSPs
   c. hyperpolarizations
   d. autoreceptors

2. The reduction of synaptic input to action potentials is:
   a. integration
   b. spatial summation
   c. temporal summation
   d. shunting

3. The nicotinic acetylcholine receptor appears to be largely selective for:
   a. calcium
   b. potassium
   c. chloride
   d. sodium

4. A drug that binds with high affinity to a receptor but has no potency would be a:
   a. agonist
   b. endogenous agonist
   c. antagonist
   d. not enough information given

5. Substances that the body manufactures are referred to as:
   a. agonists
   b. exogenous
   c. endogenous
   d. antagonists

6. A site on a receptor different from the binding site of both agonists and antagonists is called:
   a. allosteric
   b. exogenous
   c. ligand
   d. poison

7. "Vagusstoff" turned out to be:
   a. dopamine
   b. acetylcholine
   c. norepinephrine
   d. GABA

8. The amino acid precursor to the catecholamine transmitters is:
    a. glutamic acid
    b. tryptophan
    c. acetyl
    d. tyrosine

9. Parkinson's disease is due to a lack of _____ transmission in the brain.
    a. norepinephrine
    b. GABA
    c. dopamine
    d. histamine

10. Muscarinic and nicotinic are subtypes of receptors for:
    a. serotonin
    b. acetylcholine
    c. GABA
    d. dopamine

11. The compound naloxone is an:
    a. antagonist to endorphin synapses
    b. agonist at serotonin synapses
    c. endogenous transmitter
    d. agonist at endorphin synapses

12. Electrotonic synapses:
    a. are the slowest synapses
    b. do not use transmitters
    c. always use GABA as the transmitter
    d. use a variety of transmitter molecules

13. One can observe "end plates":
    a. at GABA synapses
    b. all over the brain
    c. at synapses with peptide modulators
    d. at the neuromuscular junction

14. Benzodiazapine and barbiturate drugs are:
    a. allosteric modifiers of the chloride GABA receptor
    b. serotonin receptor agonists
    c. dopaminergic antagonists
    d. inhibitory to substance P

15. Nerve gases like Sarin produce their effects by:
    a. stimulating nicotinic receptors
    b. blocking GABA inhibition
    c. blocking acetylcholinesterase
    d. blocking acetylcholine reuptake

Labeling Exercises

1. Please label these diagrams using the terms listed.

(a)

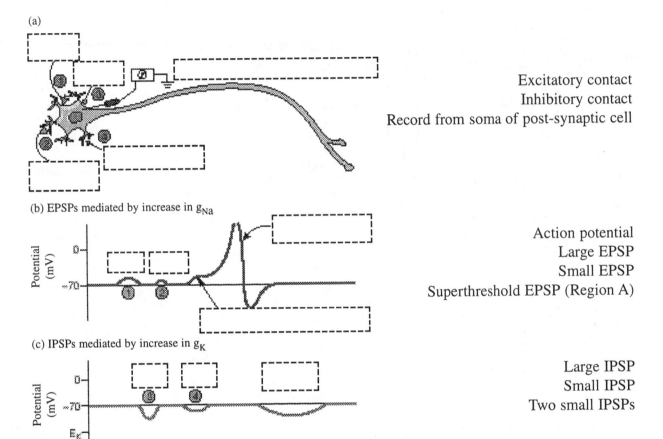

Excitatory contact
Inhibitory contact
Record from soma of post-synaptic cell

(b) EPSPs mediated by increase in g_{Na}

Action potential
Large EPSP
Small EPSP
Superthreshold EPSP (Region A)

(c) IPSPs mediated by increase in g_K

Large IPSP
Small IPSP
Two small IPSPs

2.   Please label this diagram using the terms listed.

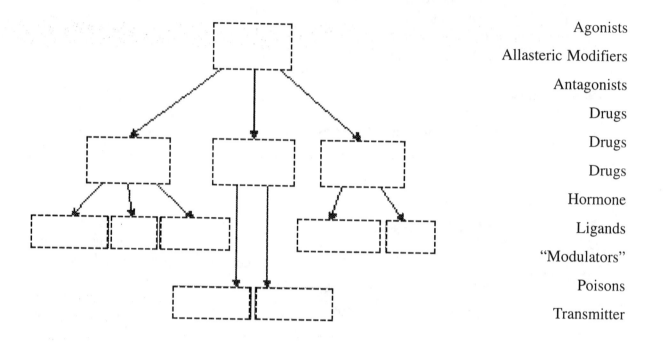

Agonists

Allasteric Modifiers

Antagonists

Drugs

Drugs

Drugs

Hormone

Ligands

"Modulators"

Poisons

Transmitter

3. Please label these diagrams using the terms listed.

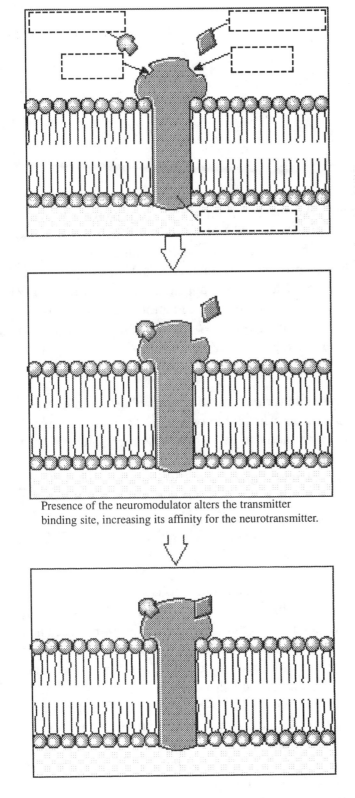

Allosteric Site
Neuromodulator
Receptor
Transmitter
Transmitter binding site

Presence of the neuromodulator alters the transmitter binding site, increasing its affinity for the neurotransmitter.

Answers

Key Terms Matching

1.	H	6.	C
2.	B	7.	E
3.	F	8.	A
4.	I	9.	D
5.	G	10.	J

Short Answer Essay Questions

1. Integration is the reduction of a large amount of input into the "decision" to either fire or not fire an action potential. A typical dendrite receives hundreds of synaptic contacts from other neurons. Some of these inputs are EPSPs, and some are IPSPs. There are two kinds of summation that cells utilize. Messages from other cells can summate over space, a process called spatial summation. By this process, two small EPSPs, for example, that alone would not be sufficient to trigger an action potential may appear at the same time and depolarize the cell to threshold. A related process is temporal summation. This refers to the fact that synaptic potentials may also summate over time. Using the same example, a small EPSP that normally would not be strong enough to trigger an action potential alone, may cause the cell to reach threshold if it appears closely in time with another small EPSP.

2. There are only two types of ligands possible for receptors. An agonist is defined as a compound that binds to a protein receptor and activates it biologically. An antagonist is a compound that binds to a receptor but does not activate it. Antagonists therefore achieve their effects by physically blocking any agonist from getting to the receptor. With some potential recent exceptions, antagonists are always exogenous substances, or compounds produced outside the body. The substances that the body produces (endogenous) that utilize a given receptor are therefore always agonists. There may, however, be more than one endogenous agonist for a receptor, and many exogenous chemicals may also function as agonists.

3. Acetylcholine, as the transmitter at the neuromuscular junction, is especially vulnerable to pharmacological manipulation. Numerous toxins exist that affect some aspect of normal cholinergic function. Several naturally-occurring toxins, such as curare from a tree and bungarotoxin from a snake are antagonists at the nicotinic cholinergic receptor. The nicotinic receptor is the receptor subtype at the neuromuscular junction. Therefore substances that block this receptor cause paralysis and eventually death via asphyxiation. Other naturally occurring compounds affect acetylcholine synapses by a completely different mechanism. Physostigmine, a natural toxin from a plant, and Sarin, a synthetic nerve gas, both block acetylcholinesterase (AchE). AchE is the synaptic enzyme that breaks down acetylcholine in the synaptic cleft. Blocking that enzyme causes an exaggeration of cholinergic transmission. This also leads to suffocation. It is an interesting fact that blocking cholinergic activity or greatly exaggerating cholinergic activity leads to death.

4. Neuromodulation is a relatively recent idea to describe how transmitter molecules may affect the activity of each other. It was discovered that each cell does not release only one transmitter molecule. Some, and perhaps most, neurons release two or more transmitter molecules. Peptide molecules appear to be very frequently used as "cotransmitters", often coreleased with more traditional molecules like dopamine or serotonin. The term neuro-modulation was proposed to describe a substance that influences the activity of another transmitter molecule. The text points out the imprecision in this statement, and proposes a better definition of neuromodulation. A neuromodulator is any substance that functions without any intrinsic effect itself, but rather allosterically modifies the affinity of a trans-mitter for a receptor. The fact that a cell can only become excited or inhibited led some early scientists to the conclusion that only two transmitter molecules were necessary. Recent dis-coveries with peptides, corelease, and neuromodulation demonstrate that the picture is much more complicated than originally thought, and will assuredly become more so.

5. An electrotonic synapse is a type of synapse that does not have a gap between neurons, and does not utilize transmitter molecules. There are channels called connexins that connect the two cells to each other. The advantage of an electrotonic synapse is speed, given that a transmitter molecule does not have to diffuse across the synaptic cleft. Although the time for diffusion is very short, it is still significantly longer than a direct connection. Logically, therefore, behaviors that have to occur very rapidly should be mediated by electrotonic synapses, and that is indeed the case. The escape response in crayfish is mediated by elec-trotonic synapses. In vertebrates, escape behaviors in fish also use electrotonic connections.

Multiple Choice Answers

1.	B	9.	C
2.	A	10.	B
3.	D	11.	A
4.	C	12.	B
5.	C	13.	D
6.	A	14.	A
7.	B	15.	C
8.	D		

The Automatic Nervous System

Chapter Summary

This chapter describes the workings of the autonomic nervous system (ANS). The ANS is the branch of the Peripheral Nervous System (PNS) that innervates internal organs, as well as glands and nonskeletal muscle throughout the body. The ANS is divided into two components, a **sympathetic division** and a **parasympathetic division**. The two divisions of the ANS are anatomically distinct, utilize different transmitter substances, and are typically functionally opposite. The two systems are also generally antagonistic, meaning that when one branch is active, the other is suppressed. Receptor proteins in the ANS are not directly associated with ion channels. Rather the transmitter initiates an intracellular cascade of events, called **second-** or even **third-messengers**. An important ANS organ is the **adrenal gland**, an important center mediating the **fight-or-flight response**. This response is a complex series of physical changes that make the body optimally prepared to deal with a physical threat. The fact that most current stressors are non-physical, yet still activate the fight-or-flight response may be a reason why stress is related to various health problems like hypertension and heart disease. There is some dispute about how autonomic or automatic the function of the ANS in fact is. Also, there are special cases, such as male sexual behavior, where a combination of sympathetic and parasympathetic activity is necessary for the behavior to occur. Each division of the ANS has a sensory component, which is poorly organized and leads to phenomena such as **referred pain**. Finally, ANS transmitter substances such as acetylcholine and norepinephrine also exist as transmitter substances in brain.

Chapter Outline:

Dual Innervation

    Opposing Systems:

        Sympathetic Division of the ANS

        Parasympathetic Division of the ANS

Anatomy

    Physical Differences:

        Preganglionic Fibers

        Postganglionic Fibers

Receptors

    Preganglionic Synapses

    Postganglionic Synapses

Nonsynaptic Release

    Second and Third Messengers

The Adrenal Gland

    Stress:

        The Fight-or-Flight Response

        Transmitters, Hormones, and Everything in Between

        Glucose Mobilization

How "Autonomic" is it?

    Box 6-1: Psychophysiology and the "Lie Detector" Test

The Special Case of Sex

The Sensory Component

    "Referred Pain"

The Enteric Nervous System and Other Simple Systems

Transmitters Common to the ANS and CNS

    Modes of Action

    Autoreceptors

    Turnover and Breakdown

    Box 6-2: Difficulties in Drug Design

    Peptide Action in Gut and Brain

Learning Objectives

After completing this chapter, you should be able to:

1. Describe how the sympathetic and parasympathetic systems are anatomically different from each other.

2. Discuss the sympathetic and parasympathetic transmitters and receptors, and how they differ from each other.

3. Describe how the ANS transmitters produce their effects by the activation of intracellular second and third messengers.

4. Describe the adrenal gland and the fight-or-flight response.

5. Discuss several transmitter substances that are common to both the ANS and the CNS.

6. Describe the enteric nervous system and other intrinsic networks of cells.

Practice Test

Key-Terms Matching

____ 1. acetylcholine	A.	short preganglionic; long postganglionic
____ 2. sympathetic	B.	parasympathetic post-ganglionic receptor type
____ 3. erection	C.	produced by parasympathetic activity
____ 4. nicotinic	D.	parasympathetic pre-ganglionic receptor type
____ 5. autoreceptors	E.	sympathetic post-ganglionic transmitter
____ 6. parasympathetic	F.	parasympathetic post-ganglionic transmitter
____ 7. enteric nervous system	G.	intrinsic nervous system of the gut
____ 8. ejaculation	H.	presynaptic receptors for the transmitter released
____ 9. muscarinic	I.	long preganglionic; short postganglionic
____ 10. norepinephrine	J.	produced by sympathetic activity

Short Answer Essay Questions

1. What are the anatomical, chemical, and functional differences between the sympathetic and parasympathetic nervous systems?

2. Is the autonomic nervous system really as "automatic" or out of one's control as has been thought?

3. What are "second" and "third messengers"? How are they different from other receptor systems?

4. What physiological changes occur during the fight-or-flight response? Why might some of these changes be related to current health problems?

5. What are two of the transmitters common to both the ANS and the CNS? Do they have similar functions in each place?

Multiple Choice Questions

1. A collection of nerve cell bodies outside the CNS is called a:
    a. ganglion
    b. nucleus
    c. fiber
    d. tract

2. Preganglionic sympathetic fibers are _____, whereas preganglionic parasympathetic fibers are _____.
    a. long; short
    b. short; short
    c. short; long
    d. long; long

3. The preganglionic transmitter for both the sympathetic and parasympathetic nervous systems is:
    a. norepinephrine
    b. epinephrine
    c. dopamine
    d. acetylcholine

4. The adrenals are so named because of their physical location, right on top of the:
    a. stomach
    b. kidneys
    c. pancreas
    d. liver

5. The enzyme phenylethanolamine N-methyltransferase converts _____ into _____.
   a. norepinephrine; epinephrine
   b. epinephrine; norepinephrine
   c. dopamine; norepinephrine
   d. norepinephrine; dopamine

6. The receptor type at all preganglionic synapses is:
   a. muscarinic cholinergic
   b. nicotinic cholinergic
   c. beta-adrenergic
   d. alpha-adrenergic

7. The enteric nervous system is the intrinsic system of the:
   a. spleen
   b. kidneys
   c. liver
   d. gut

8. The postganglionic transmitter for the sympathetic system is primarily:
   a. acetylcholine
   b. dopamine
   c. norepinephrine
   d. a & b

9. Hepatocytes are cells of the:
   a. spleen
   b. liver
   c. adrenal
   d. kidney

10. The postganglionic transmitter for the parasympathetic system is:
    a. acetylcholine
    b. dopamine
    c. norepinephrine
    d. a & b

11. Beta- and alpha-adrenergic receptors bind to:
    a. dopamine
    b. serotonin
    c. acetylcholine
    d. norepinephrine

12.   The postganglionic parasympathetic receptor is:
       a.   muscarinic cholinergic
       b.   nicotinic cholinergic
       c.   beta-adrenergic
       d.   alpha-adrenergic

13.   Erections are produced by _____ activity, while ejaculation is mediated by _____
       activity.
       a.   sympathetic; sympathetic
       b.   sympathetic; parasympathetic
       c.   parasympathetic; sympathetic
       d.   parasympathetic; parasympathetic

14.   A second messenger enzyme attached directly to the muscarinic cholinergic receptor is
       called:
       a.   inositol triphosphate
       b.   a G protein
       c.   nitric oxide
       d.   protein kinase C

15.   The polygraph test measures:
       a.   lying directly
       b.   likelihood of truth only
       c.   the persons perception of truth
       d.   physical arousal

Labeling Exercises

1.   Please complete the table using the terms listed.

Table 6-1	THE SYNAPSES OF THE AUTONOMIC NERVOUS SYSTEM		
	Preganglionic Fibers	Postganglionic Fibers	Transmitter at Target Organ
Sympathetic Division			
Parasympathetic Division			

                    acetylcholine
                    long; aminergic, a and b receptors
                    long; cholinergic, nicotinic receptors
                    norepinephrine
                    short; cholinergic, muscarinic receptors
                    short; cholinergic, nicotinic receptors

2. Please complete the table using the terms listed.

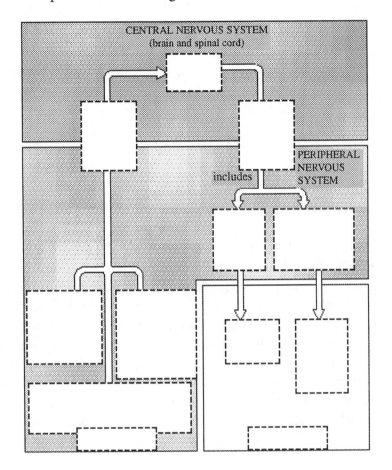

Automatic nervous system (sympathetic and parasympathetic divisions)

Cardiac muscle

Effectors

Glands

Information processing

Motor commands in efferent division

Receptors

Sensory information in afferent division

Skeletal muscle

Smooth muscle

Somatic nervous system

Somatic sensory receptors (monitor skeletal muscles, joints, skin surface, provide position sense and touch, pressure, pain and temperature sensation)

Special sensory receptors (provides sensations of smell, taste, vision, balance, and hearing)

Visceral sensory receptors (monitor internal organs, including those of cardiovascular, respiratory, digestive, urinary, and reproductive systems)

Answers

Key Terms Matching

1.	F	6.	I
2.	A	7.	G
3.	C	8.	J
4.	D	9.	B
5.	H	10.	E

Short Answer Essay Questions

1. The sympathetic and parasympathetic nervous systems are anatomically, chemically, and functionally distinct. Anatomically, there are two synaptic connections between the spinal cord and the target organ. The site of the first synapse is called a ganglion, hence we can talk about a pre-ganglionic and a post-ganglionic fiber. The sympathetic system is characterized by a short pre-ganglionic fiber, and a long post-ganglionic fiber. The parasympathetic system is the opposite, having a long pre-ganglionic fiber, and a short postganglionic fiber. The two systems are also chemically distinct, using different transmitter molecules. Both systems utilize acetylcholine as their preganglionic transmitter. They differ, however, post-ganglionically. The parasympathetic system again utilizes acetylcholine, whereas the sympathetic system uses norepinephrine. Finally, the two systems differ in their function. Sympathetic activity is generally associated with physiological arousal, whereas parasympathetic activity is associated with vegetative function or relaxation.

2. The autonomic nervous system was named under the assumption that the processes it controlled could proceed without conscious awareness of the organism, or even be controlled by the organism. That assertion has come under recent scrutiny. It is clear that genuine physical emergencies produce a sympathetic response that is clearly involuntary. Other than clear examples like that, however, the distinction between voluntary and involuntary blurs. An individual skydiving will have a sympathetic discharge that could be described as involuntary, although the behavior itself is under voluntary control (presumably). Further, there are many who believe that one can consciously control their "autonomic" responses. That question is currently being debated. If it turns out to be true, the ramifications and health benefits could be enormous, considering the number of disorders that are thought to be either caused or exacerbated by an excess of sympathetic activity.

3. Receptor systems in the ANS utilize second or third messenger systems. These are systems where the transmitter does not directly affect an ion channel, but initiates a complex chain of intracellular events that eventually impacts a channel elsewhere in the membrane. A well-described example is that of an enzyme known as a G-protein. When acetylcholine binds to the muscarinic receptor, it activates a G protein. The G protein activates a substance called phospholipace C. After several other steps, a channel completely physically separated from the receptor is affected. Systems that utilize second and third messengers

are slower than systems that directly open channels, given the time necessary for the intracellular events to occur. Their advantage, however, is that they can produce a wide range of effects on the postsynaptic cell.

4. The fight-or-flight response is a complex series of physiological changes that maximally prepare the organism for responding to a physical threat. Heartrate increases and the heart beats harder. The lungs take in more oxygen, and glucose is released into the bloodstream by the liver. The pupils dilate to perhaps improve vision. Other, "non-essential" systems such as digestion are inhibited. This is an apparent attempt to save the energy that those processes normally utilize. The entire response, as the name suggests, prepares the organism for fighting or fleeing. It is thought by many researchers that these changes that the body makes are not healthy given the kind of stressors most people face currently. Although a physical threat is still possible, the vast majority of stressors we face are psychological in nature. All of these changes, which are unnecessary for a psychological stressor, may be contributory to diseases like hypertension and heart disease.

5. Norepinephrine and acetylcholine are the two principal transmitter substances that are part of both the CNS and the ANS. It is very difficult to determine if they have similar functions in brain that they do in the periphery. Their actions are well understood in the autonomic nervous system. Brain circuits are much more complicated and much less accessible, however. Both acetylcholine and norepinephrine have been implicated in a number of behaviors. What is known is that receptor subtypes that they utilize in the periphery also exist in the brain so their actions may be similar. However, recent work using a hippocampal slice preparation indicate that the effects of acetylcholine and norepinephrine in hippocampal tissue are identical, in contrast to their opposing effects peripherally.

Multiple Choice Answers

1.	A	9.	B
2.	C	10.	A
3.	D	11.	D
4.	B	12.	A
5.	A	13.	C
6.	B	14.	B
7.	D	15.	D
8.	C		

7

The Spinal Cord

Chapter Summary

This chapter introduces the student to the structure and function of the spinal cord. Sensory fibers going towards the CNS are **afferents**. Motor fibers going away from the CNS are **efferents**. The dorsal region of the cord handles primarily sensory information, whereas the ventral region handles motor information. **White matter** in the CNS is comprised of myelinated structures like axons, while **gray matter** is composed of nonmyelinated structures like cell bodies. The body is divided into thirty one **dermatomes**, regions controlled by the thirty one pairs of spinal nerves. Many nerve fibers **decussate**, or cross over to the other side of the midline. The **first order neuron** is the first cell in the somatosensory system, and its cell body exists outside the CNS. This cell synapses with a **second order neuron** whose cell body is in the CNS. The chain continues with increasing complexity up into the brain. Motor systems are divided into **upper motor neurons**, which are completely in the CNS, and **lower motor neurons**, which leave the spinal cord and connect to the skeletal muscle. The **pyramidal** and **extrapyramidal tracts** are descending upper motor neurons that innervate the lower motor neurons. The spinal cord is able to perform a number of complex actions without any input from the brain. The **monosynaptic reflex**, for example, causes a muscle to constrict immediately after it has stretched. Also, **antagonist muscles** exist, whereby activation of one muscle causes the inhibition of its antagonist muscle. There are also two types of lower motor neurons, **alpha** and **gamma**. Gamma motor neurons innervate intrafusal fibers, which contain a muscle spindle organ. Activation of the muscle spindle organ causes the extrafusal fiber to stimulate the whole muscle to constrict. Finally, a **Renshaw Cell** causes any motor neuron that has just fired to be inhibited.

Chapter Outline

A Functional Segregation

      Afferents and Efferents:

            Orientation

            Gray Matter and White Matter

            Dermatomes

            Decussation

Sensory Pathways

      Hierarchical Organization:

            Projection of Large Mechanoreceptors

            Projection of Small Nociceptors

            Box 7-1: Brown-Sequard Syndrome

Motor Pathways

      Lower Motor Neurons

      Upper Motor Neurons

      Box 7-2: Diseases of the Upper and Lower Motor Neuron

      The "Intermediate" Horn

Integrative Circuits in the Cord

      A "Minibrain"!

      Spinal Behaviors

      The Monosynaptic Reflex

      Inhibition of Antagonist Muscles

      Alpha- and Gamma-Activation

      The Renshaw Cell

      Experimental Research

      Box 7-3: Animal Welfare and Animal Rights

Learning Objectives

After completing this chapter, you should be able to:

1. Describe how the spinal cord is functionally segregated.

2. Discuss the path of afferent information from sensory systems up to the brain.

3. Describe the path of motor commands from the brain to the muscles.

4. Describe the monosynaptic reflex.

5. Discuss how gamma and alpha motor neurons innervate muscle tissue and function to control muscle movements.

6. Describe efference copy and surround inhibition.

Practice Test

Key-Terms Matching

_____ 1. upper motor neurons

_____ 2. afferents

_____ 3. medial

_____ 4. white matter

_____ 5. alpha motor neurons

_____ 6. gamma motor neurons

_____ 7. lateral

_____ 8. efferents

_____ 9. lower motor neurons

_____ 10. gray matter

A. projections to the CNS

B. nonmyelinated structures prevail

C. farther from the midline

D. cell bodies in the ventral horn of the spinal cord

E. contact intrafusal muscle

F. contact extrafusal muscle

G. myelinated axons prevail

H. projections away from the CNS

I. close to the midline

J. cell bodies in the brain

Short Answer Essay Questions

1. What is the monosynaptic reflex?

2. What is the functional difference between the dorsal and ventral regions of the spinal cord?

3. What does a "Renshaw Cell" do?

4. What is a dermatome? What do they tell us about how the spinal cord is responsible for various parts of the body?

5. What is the path of sensory information from the sense organs to the brain?

Multiple Choice Questions

1. The portion of the body innervated by one set of spinal nerves is a:
   a. sensory root
   b. dermatome
   c. motor root
   d. segmentation

2. The most rostral segments of the spinal cord are the:
   a. cervical
   b. thoracic
   c. lumbar
   d. sacral

3. The "first cell" in any sensory system is called the:
   a. Renshaw Cell
   b. first order neuron
   c. upper neuron
   d. lower neuron

4. Second-order neurons for the mechanoreceptor system are in the:
   a. brainstem
   b. spinal cord
   c. thalamus
   d. cortex

5. The upper surface of the body is:
   a. ventral
   b. medial
   c. dorsal
   d. lateral

6. The likely transmitter in first-order nociceptors is:
   a. serotonin
   b. glycine
   c. GABA
   d. substance P

7. The ventral roots of the spinal cord are composed of primarily:
   a. motor fibers
   b. sensory fibers
   c. nociceptor fibers
   d. proprioceptor fibers

8. The "spinothalamic tract" travels from the:
   a. thalamus to the spinal cord
   b. spinal cord to the thalamus
   c. dorsal root to the pons
   d. ventral root to the pons

9. Skeletal muscles are innervated by:
   a. upper motor neurons
   b. first order neurons
   c. lower motor neurons
   d. second order neurons

10. Myelinated regions of CNS appear as:
    a. gray matter
    b. both gray and white matter
    c. neither gray nor white matter
    d. white matter

11. A lower motor neuron always uses this transmitter:
    a. glycine
    b. GABA
    c. acetylcholine
    d. substance P

12. The muscle spindle organ is located in:
    a. intrafusal fibers
    b. extrafusal fibers
    c. Renshaw Cells
    d. spinal cord

13. Extrafusal muscle is directly contacted by:
    a. gamma motor neurons
    b. alpha motor neurons
    c. Renshaw Cells
    d. muscle spindle organs

14. An interneuron that inhibits a motor neuron which has just fired is called a:
    a. pyramidal cell
    b. intrafusal fiber
    c. Renshaw Cell
    d. Golgi tendon organ

15. A pathway that crosses the midline projects:
    a. ipsilaterally
    b. medially
    c. laterally
    d. contralaterally

Labeling Exercises

1. Please label these diagrams using the terms listed.

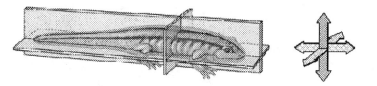

Caudal
Dorsal
Left
Right
Rostral
Ventral

Frontal (coronal) plane
Saggital plane
Transverse plane

Caudal
Dorsal
Left
Right
Rostral
Ventral

2. Please label these diagrams using the terms listed.

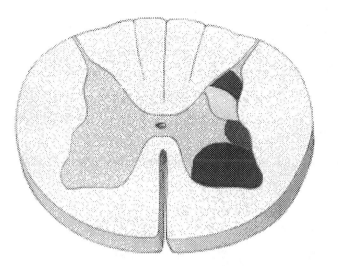

(afferent)
Dorsal gray commissure
Dorsal gray horn
Dorsal median sulcus
Dorsal white column
(efferent)
From dorsal root
Lateral white column
Lateral gray horn
Somatic motor
Somatic sensory
To ventral root
Ventral median fissure
Ventral white column
Visceral sensory
Ventral gray commissure
Ventral gray horn
Ventral white commissure
Visceral sensory

C_3
L_1
T_3

Central canal
Dorsal median sulcus
Dorsal root
Dorsal root ganglion
Gray matter
Intermediate horn
Spinal nerve
Ventral median fissure
Ventral root
White matter

 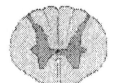

3.   Please label these diagrams using the terms listed.

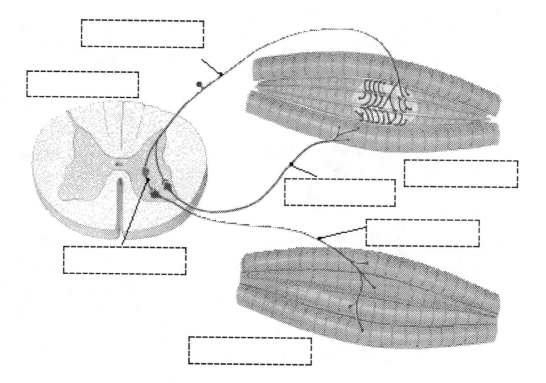

Alpha motor neuron to extensor
Alpha motor neuron to flexor
Extensor
Flexor
Inhibitory interneuron
Sensory afferent neuron
Spinal cord

Answers

Key Terms Matching

1.	J	6.	E
2.	A	7.	C
3.	I	8.	H
4.	G	9.	D
5.	F	10.	B

Short Answer Essay Questions

1. The monosynaptic reflex is a spinally mediated reflex that counters any stretch of a muscle with a constriction of that same muscle. Intrafusal fibers in muscle tissue contain a receptor sensitive to stretching of that muscle. This receptor activates a sensory neuron attached to the muscle which enters the spinal cord. This neuron synapses to a lower motor neuron which stimulates the extrafusal fibers of the same muscle, causing a contraction of that muscle. The reflex is monosynaptic because the only synapse is between the sensory afferent and the lower motor neuron in the spinal cord.

2. The spinal cord is functionally segregated between its dorsal and ventral areas. The thirty one pairs of spinal nerves bifurcate into two roots, a dorsal and a ventral root. The dorsal roots are composed primarily of sensory fibers, and the ventral roots are composed primarily of motor fibers. This division is maintained in the spinal cord, as the dorsal horn of the cord contains sensory cells, and the ventral horn contains motor cells. This segregation of function eventually disappears in brain as sensory and motor pathways merge.

3. A Renshaw Cell is a spinal interneuron that causes inhibition of a motor neuron that just fired. Motor neurons send off axon collaterals that synapse with Renshaw Cells in the cord. Renshaw Cells in turn connect back to that neuron, providing it with an inhibitory contact. In many cases, the Renshaw Cell not only inhibits the motor neuron that connects to it, but all other nearby motor neurons. This pathway is an excellent example of "efference copy," the concept of the nervous system sending a message that a command has been executed. It is also an example of how the nervous system creates contrast, by inhibiting nearby cells after a message has been received and successfully transmitted.

4. A dermatome is the region of the body controlled by one set of spinal nerves. An underappreciated fact is that humans are segmented organisms, and have thirty one dermatomes which correspond to the thirty one spinal nerves. This fact becomes readily apparent in the disease shingles. Shingles is caused by a virus which infects the spinal nerves and may exist for long periods of time in the gray matter of the spinal cord. The virus may become active and travel down the axon of one of the spinal nerves, producing a red stripe across the body corresponding to that dermatome.

5. Sensory information is first detected by first order neurons, which exist throughout the body. This is a monopolar neuron, with a neurite that extends into skin, muscle, or organ, and an axon which enters the CNS. The cell bodies of all first order neurons exist outside the CNS. The axon of the first order neuron enters the CNS and synapses with a second order neuron. The second order neuron is in the CNS. Second order neurons synapse to third order neurons on up the line. For many sensory systems, the system is fairly well understood as high up as fourth or fifth level neurons.

Multiple Choice Answers

1.	B	9.	C
2.	D	10.	D
3.	B	11.	C
4.	A	12.	A
5.	C	13.	B
6.	D	14.	C
7.	A	15.	D
8.	B		

Functional Anatomy of the Brain

Chapter Summary

This chapter introduces the student to the basic organization of the brain. The major division of the brain is between the **brainstem** and **forebrain**. There are 12 **cranial nerves**, which emanate from the brainstem and provide sensory and motor input for the head and neck. Other brainstem structures are the **medulla** and the **pons**. Three brainstem nuclei are major sources of important transmitters for the rest of the brain. The **raphe nuclei** project diffusely and are the primary source of serotonin for the brain. Similarly, the **locus coeruleus** is the major source of norepinephrine, and the **substantia nigra** is a major source of dopamine. The **basal ganglia** is comprised of the **caudate nucleus**, the **putamen**, and the **globus pallidus**, and is an important part of the extrapyramidal motor system. The **limbic system** is another forebrain area that appears to be involved in the expression of emotion. The **hypothalamus** is a forebrain structure important for feeding, sexual behavior, and a number of other behaviors partially via its control of the **pituitary gland**, the structure inferior to it. The most central region of the forebrain is the **thalamus**, which contains relay nuclei for sensory information and association nuclei. The largest part of the brain is **neocortex**, composed of two heavily convoluted hemispheres. The cortex is divided into four geographic lobes, the **frontal**, **parietal**, **temporal**, and **occipital**, based on location and function. The brain also contains a **ventricular system**, which is filled with **cerebrospinal fluid**. The brain receives protection from the **meninges,** and the **blood-brain-barrier**. Finally, much of our knowledge of brain anatomy comes from lesion studies, as well as studies using radioactively labeled compounds.

Chapter Outline

Orientation

Gross Subdivisions of the Brain

     Brainstem and Forebrain:

          Cranial Nerves

          Box 8-1: Bell's Palsy and Carpal Tunnel Syndrome

          Brainstem

Brainstem Projections to Forebrain

     Sources of Transmitter:

          Raphe Nuclei

          Locus Coeruleus

          Substantia Nigra

Basal Ganglia

     Extrapyramidal Motor System:

          Limbic System

     Emotion:

          Box 8-2: The "Hierarchy of Being"

Hypothalamus and Pituitary

     Anterior and Posterior regions:

Thalamus

     Center of the Forebrain:

          Relay Nuclei

          Association Nuclei

Neocortex

    Two Hemispheres:

        Primary Cortex

        Association Cortex

        Temporal Lobes

        Occipital Lobes

        Parietal Lobes

        Frontal Lobes

        Box 8-3: Frontal Lobotomy

Other Neocortex

    Box 8-4: Pseudoscience

Ventricles

Meninges and the Blood-Brain Barrier

    Protecting the brain:

        Tract-Tracing Techniques and Stereotaxy

Learning Objectives

After competing this chapter, you should be able to:

1. Describe the functions of the 12 cranial nerves.

2. Elucidate the location and function of the raphe nuclei, the locus coeruleus, and the substantia nigra.

3. Discuss the structure and function of the basal ganglia.

4. Describe the four lobes of the cortex and their function.

5. Describe how lesion and tracing studies can inform us about pathways in the brain.

6. Describe the structures and function of the limbic system.

Practice Test

Key-Terms Matching

_____ 1. parietal lobe   A. primary auditory cortex

_____ 2. locus coeruleus   B. primary somatosensory cortex

_____ 3. LGN   C. major source of dopamine

_____ 4. frontal lobe   D. relay auditory information

_____ 5. thalamus   E. primary source of norepinephrine

_____ 6. MGN   F. primary visual cortex

_____ 7. temporal lobe   G. relay visual information

_____ 8. raphe nuclei   H. most central structure of the forebrain

_____ 9. occipital lobe   I. primary source of serotonin

_____10. substantia nigra   J. ideation and cognition

Short Answer Essay Questions

1. What are the two major kinds of thalamic nuclei, and what are their functions?

2. What structures comprise the limbic system? What functions does this system seem to control?

3. What are cranial nerves and what are their function?

4. What are the four primary regions of cortex and what are their functions?

5. What are the three groups of cells in the brainstem that provide the rest of the brain with three major transmitters?

Multiple Choice

1. The most caudal structure in the brainstem is the:
   a. pons
   b. metencephalon
   c. tectum
   d. medulla

2. The three oculomotor cranial nerves all control:
   a. eye movement
   b. vision
   c. audition
   d. spatial perception

3. Temporal-mandibular joint (TMJ) pain arises from irritation of this nerve:
   a. abducens
   b. trigeminal
   c. facial
   d. glossopharyngeal

4. The dorsal regions of the tectum that handle visual information are the:
   a. inferior colliculi
   b. superior colliculi
   c. cerebellar peduncles
   d. pontine nuclei

5. The major source of norepinephrine for the brain comes from the:
   a. raphe nuclei
   b. substantia nigra
   c. locus coeruleus
   d. none of the above

6. The caudate nucleus, putamen, and globus pallidus comprise the:
   a. basal ganglia
   b. substantia nigra
   c. tectum
   d. limbic system

7. Limbic damage produces an animal that is abnormal in:
   a. vision
   b. movement
   c. autonomic function
   d. emotion

8.   The lateral and medial geniculate nuclei are sensory relay nuclei of the:
     a. hypothalamus
     b. pituitary
     c. halamus
     d. basal ganglia

9.   Cortex that receives a direct projection from a sensory relay nucleus is called:
     a. first order cortex
     b. primary cortex
     c. tertiary cortex
     d. secondary cortex

10. The major source of serotonin for the brain comes from the:
     a. raphe nuclei
     b. substantia nigra
     c. locus coeruleus
     d. none of the above

11. The primary visual cortex is in this lobe:
     a. frontal
     b. parietal
     c. occipital
     d. temporal

12. The gyrus immediately rostral to the central sulcus is the:
     a. postcentral gyrus
     b. paracentral gyrus
     c. calcarine gyrus
     d. precentral gyrus

13. Cerebrospinal fluid is manufactured in the:
     a. calcarine sulcus
     b. tectum
     c. choroid plexus
     d. central canal

14. The outermost layer of the meninges is the:
     a. pia mater
     b. dura mater
     c. CSF
     d. arachnoid

15. Damage to cell bodies leads to degeneration of distal structures like axons. This is called:
    a. retrograde degeneration
    b. anterograde degeneration
    c. retroactive degeneration
    d. orthograde degeneration

Labeling Exercises

1. Please label this diagram using the terms listed.

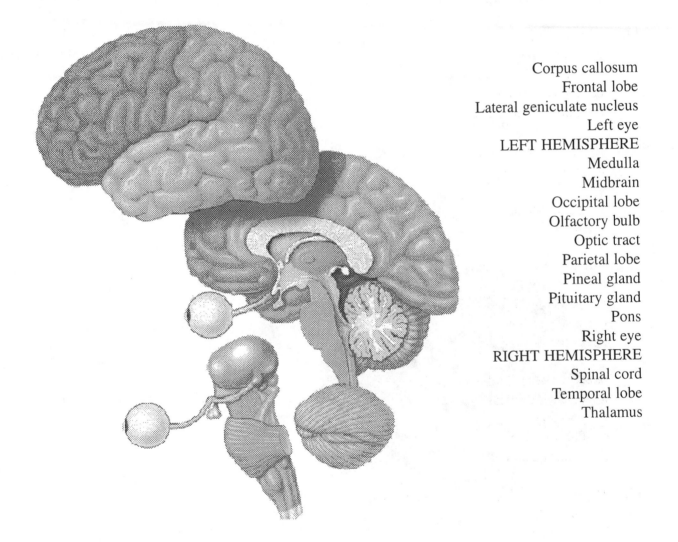

Corpus callosum
Frontal lobe
Lateral geniculate nucleus
Left eye
LEFT HEMISPHERE
Medulla
Midbrain
Occipital lobe
Olfactory bulb
Optic tract
Parietal lobe
Pineal gland
Pituitary gland
Pons
Right eye
RIGHT HEMISPHERE
Spinal cord
Temporal lobe
Thalamus

2.   Please label these diagrams using the terms listed.

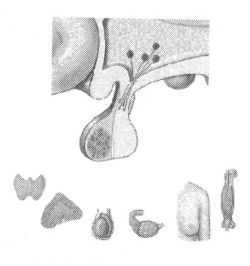

Anterior pituitary hormones
Anteriorpituitary
TSH
ACTH
FSH & LH
Prolactin
GH
Thyroid
Adrenal cortex
Testis
Ovary
Mammary glands
Bone and muscle organs

3.   Please label these diagrams using the terms listed.

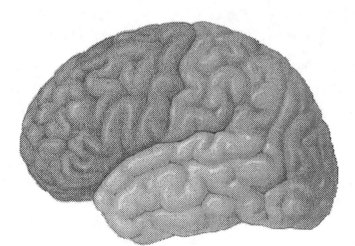

Frontal lobe
Occipital lobe
Parietal lobe
Temporal lobe

Answers

Key Terms Matching

1. B
2. E
3. G
4. J
5. H

6. D
7. A
8. I
9. F
10. C

Short Answer Essay Questions

1. The thalamus is in some sense the connection between the "old" and "new"brain. It contains two major kinds of nuclei, relay nuclei and association nuclei. Relay nuclei receive ascending input from specific sensory systems and then transmit (or relay) that information up to the appropriate cortical region. An example is the lateral geniculate nucleus (LGN) which receives visual information from the retina, and transmits it up to the visual cortex. The second major type of thalamic nucleus are association nuclei. These are areas that don't have a known sensory or motor function. The distinction between relay and association nuclei may have more to do with our lack of knowledge than any real difference.

2. The limbic system is a group of structures that include the amygdala, the mammillary bodies, the olfactory bulbs, the septum, the hippocampus, and the habenula. All of these structures can be assigned to other systems as well, which makes the elucidation of the function of the limbic system difficult. Old research indicated that damage to limbic areas produced no obvious detriments in sensory, autonomic, or motor function. Therefore the limbic system does not have a controlling function to these phenomena. Subjects with limbic damage appeared to react to stimuli with abnormal emotional responses. The limbic system, therefore, appears to contribute to the normal expression of affect.

3. The twelve pairs of cranial nerves are analogous to the thirty one pairs of spinal nerves, but they control sensory and motor function of the head and neck. Some are completely sensory in nature, like the optic and olfactory nerves. Others are completely motor, such as the oculomotor nerve, which contributes to the movement of the eyes. Some are mixed, having a partly sensory and partly motor function. An example of a mixed cranial nerve is the trigeminal, which relays sensory information from the mouth and face but also carries axons of motor nerves that control chewing. Finally, the nerves also provide most of the preganglionic parasympathetic fibers for the entire body.

4. The neocortex is divided into four lobes based on location. These four areas also differ functionally. Most caudally are located in the occipital lobe. In the occipital lobes are the primary visual cortex, where projections from the LGN terminate. Caudal to the central sulcus on the dorsal surface of the brain are the parietal lobes. The first gyrus of the parietal lobes is the postcentral gyrus, which functions as the primary somatosensory cortex. The

temporal lobes are separated from the rest of the cortex by the lateral sulcus, and contain the primary auditory cortex, which receives projections from the MGN. Finally, rostral to the central sulcus is the frontal lobe. The most caudal gyrus in the frontal lobe is the precentral gyrus, which is the primary motor cortex.

5.   Among the many brainstem nuclei that perform a variety of functions are three nuclei that are major sources of monoamine transmitters. The raphe nuclei are a series of nuclei on the midline which are the major source of serotonin for the brain. The raphe project diffusely throughout the cortex and rest of brain. The locus coeruleus, Latin for blue spot, is a structure lateral to the dorsal pons. It appears to be the major source of norepinephrine for the brain. Analogous to the serotinergic raphe projections, the locus coeruleus also projects diffusely throughout the brain. Finally, the substantia nigra is a structure in the ventral brainstem. It is one, although not the only, source of dopamine. The substantia nigra projects to the basal ganglia and has an important role in motor behavior.

Multiple Choice Answers

1.	D	9.	B
2.	A	10.	A
3.	B	11.	C
4.	B	12.	D
5.	C	13.	C
6.	A	14.	B
7.	D	15.	D
8.	C		

Sensory Systems

Chapter Summary

This chapter introduces the student to sensation and sensory systems. **Somatosensation**, or information from the body, comes from several closely related systems. Primary sensory neurons don't produce synaptic potentials, but rather exhibit **generator potentials**, which are graded in intensity in response to the intensity of the stimulus. Primary sensory neurons also exhibit **adaptation**, meaning the cell stops responding to a constant stimulus until it terminates. The mammalian auditory system consists of three parts. An outer ear, or **pinna,** is separated from the middle ear by the **tympanic membrane**. This membrane connects to three small bones called the **malleus**, the **incus**, and the **stapes**. These bones connect to the oval window which connects to the inner ear. In the inner ear, the **cochlea** contains the **basilar membrane**, which contains the actual receptors for hearing. The auditory system codes for the frequency of the auditory by several techniques. **Olfaction** and **gustation** are two closely related senses. The organs for taste, **taste buds**, are on the tongue, and there are at least four. Four taste receptors have been identified, for bitter, sour, salty, and sweet tastes. Primary olfactory neurons are called **bipolar cells**, and exist **olfactory epithelium**. The visual system is the most studied and best understood of the sensory systems. The back of the eye, or **retina**, contains the two kinds of **photoreceptors, rods** and **cones**. These cells convert or **transduce** light into neural impulses. Transduction occurs via photopigments. Cells in the visual system also have **receptive fields**, or areas of the visual world that they are responsible for. These fields tend to have a circular segment with an outer ring. Visual information projects ultimately to the **primary visual cortex** in the occipital lobe, where it is analyzed by **simple cells**, as well as more complex cells.

Chapter Outline

Somatosensory Systems

    Information from the body:

        Organs of Touch

        Adaptation and Generator Potentials

        Central Projections

        Box 9-1: Homunculi

        Proprioceptors and Their Projections

Auditory System

    Organs of Hearing

    Hindbrain Projections

    Thalamic and Cortical Projections

    Efferent Projections

    Box 9-2: "The Cocktail Party Phenomenon"

    Vestibular System and its Projections

Olfaction and Gustation

    Closely Related Senses

    Organs of Taste

    Organs of Smell

    Central Projections

Vision

    Anatomy and Circuitry of the Retina

    Transduction of the Light Stimulus

    Surround Inhibition

    Thalamic and Brainstem Projections

    Cortical Circuits and Columns

Box 9-3: Serial or Parallel Processing

    Association Visual Cortex

    Diagnostic Neurology of the Visual System

Six Principles of Sensory Physiology

Learning Objectives

After completing this chapter, you should be able to:

1. Describe sensory adaptation and its purpose.

2. Elucidate the important structures of the auditory system.

3. Describe the path of visual information from the level of the photoreceptors to the LGN.

4. Describe the six rules of sensory physiology.

5. Discuss the process of transduction, using rhodopsin as an example.

Practice Test

Key-Terms Matching

____	1.	medial geniculate	A.	optic nerve decussation
____	2.	transduction	B.	inability to smell
____	3.	eardrum	C.	temporal lobe
____	4.	primary auditory cortex	D.	auditory relay nucleus
____	5.	olfactory nerve	E.	carries gustatory information
____	6.	facial nerve	F.	carries olfactory information
____	7.	optic chiasm	G.	translation of sensory input into neural energy
____	8.	anosmia	H.	visual relay nucleus
____	9.	primary visual cortex	I.	occipital lobe
____	10.	lateral geniculate	J.	tympanic membrane

Short Answer Essay Questions

1. What is sensory adaptation? What is its function?

2. How is sound frequency coded by the auditory system?

3. What are the major cell types in the retina?

4. What is a simple cell? How are simple cells aligned in visual cortex?

5. How many taste receptors exist? How do these produce the sensations of thousands of tastes?

Multiple Choice

1. Stimulus intensity in sensory systems is coded for by:
   a. GABA inhibition
   b. generator potentials
   c. action potential frequency
   d. Cl- flux

2. The visible portion of the mammalian ear is called the:
   a. pinna
   b. eardrum
   c. tympanic membrane
   d. pacinian corpuscle

3. The depolarization at the neurite of a primary sensory neuron is called a(n):
   a. action potential
   b. transduction
   c. end plate potential
   d. generator potential

4. The middle and outer ears are separated by the:
   a. ossicles
   b. tympanic membrane
   c. basilar membrane
   d. cochlea

5. The ossicles cause this membrane to vibrate the:
   a. tympanic membrane
   b. oval window
   c. cochlea
   d. vestibular apparatus

6. The utricle and saccule are parts of the:
   a. vestibular system
   b. auditory system
   c. visual system
   d. gustatory system

7. The rearmost part of the tongue is where perception of _____ tastes arise:
   a. salty
   b. sweet
   c. bitter
   d. sour

8. The olfactory epithelium contains the:
   a. cribriform plate
   b. secondary olfactory cells
   c. paleocortex
   d. primary olfactory cells

9. Rods and cones both project to:
   a. amacrine cells
   b. photoreceptor cells
   c. bipolar cells
   d. ganglion cells

10. Rhodopsin is the:
    a. photopigment for short-wavelength cones
    b. photopigment for rods
    c. photopigment for long-wavelength cones
    d. photopigment for all cones

11. The area of the visual world that a given cell is responsible for is its:
    a. receptive field
    b. annulus
    c. retinotopic map
    d. homunculus

12. The half of the retina next to the temples is the:
    a. decussation
    b. nasal hemiretina
    c. optic tract
    d. temporal hemiretina

13. Cells in the LGN that are concerned primarily with detection of movement are the:
    a. parvocellular layers
    b. optic radiations
    c. magnocellular layers
    d. optic tectums

14. Cells in the striate cortex that respond to edges of light in a particular orientation are:
    a. simple cells
    b. grandmother cells
    c. complex cells
    d. hypercomplex cells

15. A homunculus is a/an:
    a. first order proprioceptor
    b. neural map of the body
    c. afferent auditory projection
    d. second order ganglion cell

Labeling Exercises

1. Please label these diagrams using the terms listed.

Auditory tube
Branch of N VII (cut)
External auditory canal
Footplate of stapes in oval win-
dow
Incus
Malleus
Round window
Stapes
Stapedius muscle
Temporal bone
Tensor tympani muscle
Tympanic membrane (tympa-
num)

Auditory ossicles
Auditory tube
Bony labyrinth of inner ear
Cartilage
Cochlea
External auditory canal
EXTERNAL EAR
Facial nerve (N VII)
INNER EAR
Internal jugular vein
MIDDLE EAR
Oval window
Pinna
Round window
Temporal bone (petrous portion)
To pharynx
Tympanic membrane
Vestibulocochlear nerve (N VIII)

Anterior
Cochlea
Cochlear duct
Cristae within ampullae
Lateral
Macula
Organ of Corti
Posterior
Saccule
Semicircular canal
Semicircular ducts
Tympanic duct
Utricle
Vestibular duct
Vestibule

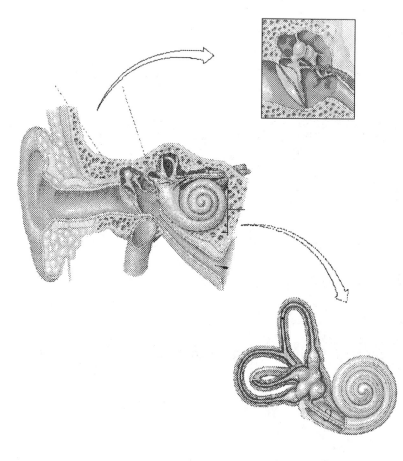

2. Please label these diagrams using the terms listed.

Basilar membrane   Cochlear nerve   Scala Vestibuli   Vestibular membrane
Bony cochlear wall   Organ of Corti   Spiral ganglion
Cochlear duct   Scala tympani   Tectorial membrane

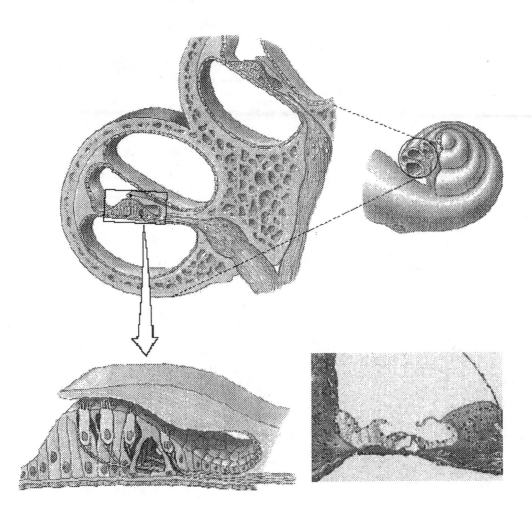

Basilar membrane   Basilar membrane
Inner hair cell   Cochlear duct (scala media)
Nerve fibers   Hair cells of organ of Corti
Outer hair cell   Spiral ganglion cells of cochlear nerve
Tectorial membrane   Tectorial membrane
                                    Tympanic duct (scala tympani)
                                    Vestibular membrane

3.   Please label these diagrams using the terms listed.

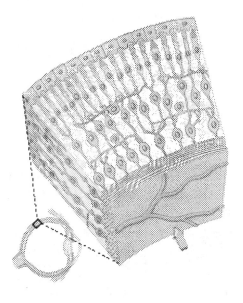
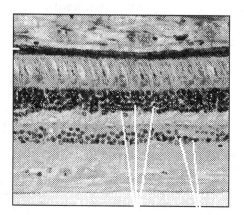

Amacrine cell	Choroid
Bipolar cells	Nuclei of bipolar cells
Cone	Nuclei of ganglion cells
Ganglion cells	Nuclei of rods and cones
Horizontal cell	Posterior cavity
Light	Rods and cones
Pigmented layer of retina	

Answers

Key Terms Matching

1.	D	6.	E
2.	G	7.	A
3.	J	8.	B
4.	C	9.	I
5.	F	10.	H

Short Answer Essay Questions

1. Sensory adaptation is the fact that a stimulus that is constant and unchanging will not be consciously noticed. An excellent example of this is in the somatosensory system. Pressure to a part of the body will produce a generator potential, that will terminate, even if the stimulus continues. The removal of the stimulus will produce another generator potential, but none during the interim. The apparent purpose of adaptation is to reduce the amount of information getting into conscious awareness. If we were forced to constantly attend to all of the sensory information coming in from all of the different modalities, thought itself would probably be incredibly difficult, or even impossible!

2. The auditory system codes for the frequency of auditory stimuli in two major ways. The human auditory system is sensitive to stimuli in the range of 20 to 20,000 HZ (cycles per second). For sounds of low frequency, up to about 5000 HZ, the action potentials match the frequency of the sound wave. In other words, a 3000 HZ sound wave will cause 3000 action potentials per second in the cochlea. At frequencies higher than 5000 HZ, the cells cannot keep up, given their refractory periods. Therefore, another strategy must be adopted. At these higher frequencies, a volley principle takes over, meaning that ganglion cells fire at different times in a volley, to match the frequency of the sound wave.

3. The back of the eye, or retina, contains five major cell types. First are the rods and cones, which are the photoreceptor cells. These are the cells that contain the photopigment molecules, where transduction occurs. Rods and cones synapse onto bipolar cells, which in turn synapse onto ganglion cells. Axons of ganglion cells leave the back of the eye as the optic nerve. There are two other major cell types in the retina, apart from this "linear" pathway of information. Rods and cones also synapse onto horizontal cells, so named because they are perpendicular to the rods, cones, and bipolar cells. Finally, amacrine cells exist between the bipolar and ganglion cells, and are also perpendicular to the cells in the "linear" pathway.

4. Hubel and Wiesel won the Noble prize for their serendipitous discovery of simple cells in primary visual cortex. They were recording from cats when they found a cell that would only fire when the cat was presented with a bar or edge in a particular orientation. As the bar was distorted from the preferred orientation, the cell would fire less and less. Hubel and

Wiesel named these cells "simple cells" because they had the simplest response characteristics of all of the cells they studied in striate cortex. They also found that the preferred orientation that excited the simple cells changed as one moved around the primary visual cortex. This appears to mean that at one level of analysis, the visual cortex maps the visual world based on edges that are perceived.

5.   The exact number of taste receptors that exist are still a mystery to researchers. However, four kinds of taste buds have been extensively studied. These are receptors for the tastes of sweet, salty, bitter, and sour. Sweet flavors are perceived by the front of the tongue, salty and sour tastes by the middle of the tongue. Bitter tastes are perceived by the very back of the tongue. Although it is not known exactly how many specific taste receptors exist, it is almost certainly true that the thousands of tastes we can perceive are produced by some combination of stimulation of a lesser number of taste bud types.

Multiple Choice Answers

1.	C	9.	C
2.	A	10.	B
3.	D	11.	A
4.	B	12.	D
5.	B	13.	C
6.	A	14.	A
7.	C	15.	B
8.	D		

$\boldsymbol{10}$

Motor Systems

Chapter Summary

This chapter introduces the student to motor systems. The **psychomotor cortex** is a group of cortical areas that contribute to motor movements. The **cingulate gyrus, supplementary motor area**, and **premotor cortex** are all involved in planning movements. The information is then relayed to the **primary motor cortex (PMC)** for execution of the movement. The PMC contains a **homunculus**, or map of the body surface. Betz cells, giant pyramidal cells in the PMC combine with other fibers to become the descending **pyramidal tracts**. Another motor system is the **extrapyramidal system**, which includes structures like the **basal ganglia, thalamus**, and **cerebellum**. The basal ganglia are a group of subcortical structures that appear to contribute to volitional aspects of movement. This is believed in large part because two diseases of the basal ganglia, **Parkinson's** and **Huntington's**, are characterized by a lack of voluntary movements, and involuntary movements, respectively. The cerebellum appears to function more to refine the execution of motor movements. It receives three major afferents and also sends three major efferent pathways. The output of the cerebellum is apparently inhibitory in nature. The importance of inhibition is dramatically illustrated by the **epileptic disorders**, a group of disorders characterized by seizures as a manifestation. Simple organisms with relatively simple nervous systems often exhibit **eutely**, meaning each member of the species has the exact same number of neurons. These eutelous systems often produce **fixed action patterns**, which are complex stereotypic behaviors elicited by a specific type of stimulus.

Chapter Outline

The Frontal and Parietal Lobes

"Psychomotor" Cortex

The Motor Homunculus

Primary Motor Cortex

Box 10-1: Intention, Volition, and "Free Will"

The Basal Ganglia

Caudate, Putamen, and Globus Pallidus

The Pathobiology of Stroke and Diseases of the Basal Ganglia

The Cerebellum

Afferents

Efferents

Box 10-2: The Cerebellum as a Vector Analyzer

Intrinsic Circuitry

The Importance of Inhibition

Efference Copy in the Oculomotor System

Box 10-3: An Experiment in Efference Copy

Epilepsy and Seizures

Command Neurons and Motor Tapes

Learning Objectives

After competing this chapter, you should be able to:

1. Describe the parts of the psychomotor cortex.

2. Discuss the structures of the pyramidal tracts and the extrapyramidal system.

3. Describe Parkinson's and Huntington's diseases, and discuss what structures are affected.

4. Elucidate the inputs and outputs of the cerebellum.

5. Describe the importance of inhibition in motor control.

6. Describe eutely, fixed action patterns, and motor tapes.

Practice Test

Key-Terms Matching

_____ 1. Betz cells

A. caudate and putamen

_____ 2. hypoxia

B. loss of blood flow

_____ 3. striatum

C. partial paralysis

_____ 4. petit mal seizures

D. motor homunculus

_____ 5. precentral gyrus

E. phylogenetically oldest part of the cerebellum

_____ 6. clonus

F. absence seizures

_____ 7. tonus

G. dramatic jerking movements

_____ 8. hemiplegia

H. forceful muscle constrictions

_____ 9. vestibulocerebellum

I. inadequate oxygen

_____10. ischemia

J. giant pyramidal cells in PMC

Short Answer Essay Questions

1. What are the three types of eye movements made when the head is still?

2. What structures comprise the basal ganglia? What does its function appear to be?

3. Where is the primary motor cortex? What does the body map look like there?

4. What are the three major inputs to the cerebellum?

5. Where does the "decision" to move come from?

Multiple Choice Questions

1. The phylogenetically oldest part of the cerebellum is the:
   a. neocerebellum
   b. corticocerebellum
   c. mesocerebellum
   d. vestibulocerebellum

2. The premotor cortex is in the:
    a. frontal lobe
    b. parietal lobe
    c. temporal lobe
    d. occipital lobe

3. Within the basal ganglia, the striatum projects to the:
    a. caudate nucleus
    b. putamen
    c. globus pallidus
    d. internal capsule

4. Akinesia is the:
    a. inability to stop movement
    b. inability to initiate movement
    c. inability to stop movement
    d. inability to change directions

5. Parkinson's patients lack the transmitter:
    a. norepinephrine
    b. dopamine
    c. GABA
    d. glycine

6. The cerebellum has this many cell layers:
    a. 2
    b. 6
    c. 4
    d. 3

7. The principle cell type in the cerebellum is the:
    a. Purkinje cell
    b. Golgi cell
    c. basket cell
    d. stellate cell

8. Eye movements where the two eyes move in opposite directions are called:
    a. saccades
    b. optokinetic movements
    c. vergence movements
    d. pursuit movements

9. Behaviors "released" by a sensory stimulus which play out in very stereotypic fashion are:
   a. motor tapes
   b. fixed action patterns
   c. command actions
   d. reflexes

10. Escape behaviors in fish and other amphibians are organized by:
    a. basket cells
    b. Purkinje cells
    c. eutelous cells
    d. Mauthner cells

11. The hypothetical motor analogue to the sensory "grandmother cell" is the:
    a. basket cell
    b. command neuron
    c. Mauthner cell
    d. Purkinje cell

12. The area of the limbic system that projects to the premotor cortex and SMA and influences the plan for action is the:
    a. cingulate gyrus
    b. hippocampus
    c. psychomotor cortex
    d. putamen

13. Huntington's disease sufferers exhibit "choreas," which are:
    a. hemiparalysis
    b. lack of motor movements
    c. sudden limb movements
    d. inability to initiate movements

14. "Cerebellar ataxia" is:
    a. sudden limb movements
    b. inability to initiate motor movements
    c. lack of motor sequences
    d. loss of muscle coordination after cerebellar damage

15. Small, darting eye movements are:
    a. smooth pursuits
    b. vestibulo-ocular pursuits
    c. saccades
    d. frontal eye fields

Chapter 10   Motor Systems

Labeling Exercises

1. Please label this diagram using the terms listed.

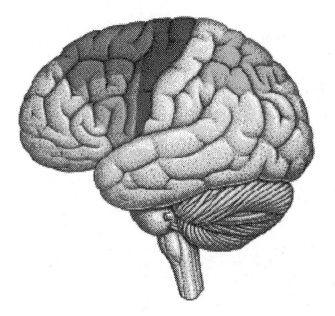

Prefrontal cortex
Premotor cortex
Primary motor cortex
Primary somatic sensory cortex
Posterior parietal cortex
Supplementary motor area (SMA)

2. Please label the diagram using the terms listed.

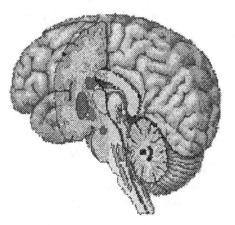

Basal ganglia
Caudate nucleus
Cingulate gyrus
Globus pallidus
Motor cortex
Putamen
Red nucleus
Thalamus

3.   Please label the diagram using the terms listed.

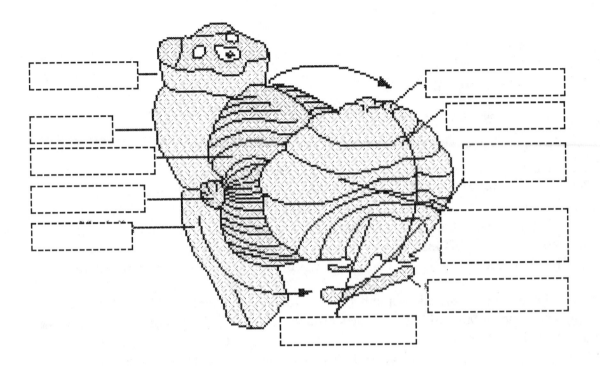

Anterior lobe	Medulla	Spinocerebellum
Cerebellum	Midbrain	Two cerebeller Hemispheres
Corticocerebelum	Pons	Vestibulocerebellum
Flocculus	Posterior lobe	

Answers

Key Terms Matching

1.	J	6.	G
2.	I	7.	H
3.	A	8.	C
4.	F	9.	E
5.	D	10.	B

Short Answer Essay Questions

1. The eyes make three basic kinds of movements when the heads is still. Saccades are small, reflexive darting movements. Both eyes move in the same direction during saccades. A second kind of movement is smooth pursuit. Smooth pursuit involves the eyes also moving in tandem, but this time to track an object that is moving. The final kind of movement is a vergence movement. In this kind of movement, the eyes move in different directions. This final type of eye movement is also controlled by a different neural system than the first two.

2. The basal ganglia is a collection of subcortical structures that include the caudate nucleus, the putamen, the globus pallidus, and the substantia nigra. These structures are part of the extrapyramidal motor system, and seem to be involved in the volitional aspect of motor behavior. A major reason for this assertion is that damage or disease to the basal ganglia produces problems with voluntary movement. Parkinson's disease is a degenerative disorder where a patient loses dopamine-producing cells in the substantia nigra. A primary symptom of Parkinson's is a deficit in the initiation of voluntary movements. Huntington's disease is a disorder that affects a different part of the basal ganglia. This disorder is characterized by choreas, which are involuntary motor movements.

3. The primary motor cortex (PMC) is a strip of cortex that is immediately anterior to the central sulcus. It is therefore the precentral gyrus, or the "last" gyrus of the frontal lobe. The PMC is somatotopically organized, meaning that different parts of the body are represented on different parts of the gyrus. The representation of different body parts into a little "person" is called a homunculus. The motor homunculus on the PMC is a strange looking person with abnormally large hands, face and tongue. This is because the parts of the body that require fine motor control, like the aforementioned regions, have more PMC devoted to them. The areas that require less motor control have less cortical area controlling them.

4. The cerebellum has three major afferents into it, which enter into three distinct subregions. The first afferent enters the oldest part of the cerebellum, the vestibulocerebellum. As the name implies, the input comes from the vestibular organs. The second major afferent comes from proprioceptors in the spinal cord as well as sensory information from the cranial nerves. This input enters the region of the cerebellum called the spinocerebellum. The third and final afferent enters the corticocerebellum. As the name implies, this input comes primarily from cortex, in particular from the extrapyramidal motor cortex.

5. Localization of the neural area that controls the decision to move is an interesting problem. A modern approach is to use noninvasive recording techniques on live subjects that detect metabolically active brain regions. Using this technology can potentially allow us to see what areas "light up" during and before movements. If a human volunteer is asked to flex a finger, for example, an increase in metabolic activity is observed in the contralateral primary motor cortex where the hand is controlled. When a more complex motor task is requested, activity also increases in the supplementary motor cortex. Most interestingly, when the subject is asked to just mentally rehearse the act but not perform it, the supplementary area alone shows an increase in activity. These data appear to suggest that the decision to act, at least for some movements, may exist somewhere between the supplementary motor cortex, and the PMC.

Multiple Choice Answers

1.	D	9.	B
2.	A	10.	D
3.	C	11.	B
4.	B	12.	A
5.	B	13.	C
6.	D	14.	D
7.	A	15.	C
8.	C		

Pleasure and Pain

Chapter Summary

This chapter introduces the student to the concepts of **pleasure** and **pain**, difficult concepts to define. There are probably several pleasure circuits in the brain, but the best understood employ either **dopamine** or **endogenous opiate** molecules as transmitters. Olds and Milner discovered in the 1950s that animals would press a lever to receive electrical stimulation in various parts of the brain. The area that produced the best responding was called the **medial forebrain bundle**, which projects from hindbrain to various sites, most notably the **nucleus accumbens**. The medial forebrain bundle appears to be primarily dopaminergic, and that transmitter has been implicated in biological **reward** as well as in the action of addictive narcotics. Tissue damage to an area of the body causes the release of the molecules **histamine** and **bradykinin**. Two kinds of fibers, **C-fibers** and **A-delta** fibers, carry nociceptive information centrally. These primary nociceptors utilize **Substance P** as their transmitter. Second-order nociceptors carry information upwards via the **lateral spinothalamic tract**. Pain does show adaptation like other senses, but also shows the opposite, **summation**, meaning a constant stimulus becomes more painful. There is a descending pathway called the **dorsolateral funiculus**, which produces **analgesia**, or insensitivity to pain if it is stimulated. It is also known that there are endogenous opiate molecules in the brain and spinal cord which mediate the analgesia produced by dorsolateral funiculus stimulation. **Gate-control theory** postulates that there is a neural gate in the spinal cord for pain that can be opened or closed by a variety of stimuli. Finally, under conditions of stress, people and animals are much less sensitive to pain, a phenomena known as **stress-induced analgesia**. This phenomena is presumably mediated by a combination of opioid and nonopioid mechanisms.

Chapter Outline

The Problem of Definitions

Is There a "Pleasure Circuit" in the Brain?

    Self-Stimulation Studies

    Box 11-1: Motivation and "Drive"

    The Medial Forebrain Bundle

    Dopamine and Reward Systems

Ascending Nociceptor Systems

    The Beginning of Pain:

        Substance P

        Box 11-2: "Dale's Law"

        The Spinothalamic Tract

        Pain and the "Six Principles" of Sensory Physiology

Descending Analgesia Systems

    Stopping Pain:

        Enkephalins and Endorphins

The Mechanism of Opioid Peptide Action

    The Raphe Nuclei

    The Periaqueductal gray

    A Final Common Pathway

    Box 11-3: Chronic Pain and Stimulation-Produced Analgesia

    Acupuncture

    Stress-Induced Analgesia

    Box 11-4: Placebo and Opioid Peptides

Learning Objectives

After competing this chapter, you should be able to:

1. Describe the studies of self-stimulation and discuss the role of dopamine.

2. Discuss how pain compares to other sensory systems with regard to the "six principles" of sensory physiology.

3. Describe the mechanism of action of the opioid peptides.

4. Discuss gate control theory.

5. Describe the pathway of nociceptive information from the first-order cell up to the thalamus.

6. Elucidate how stimulation-induced analgesia can be used to treat chronic pain patients.

Practice Test

Key-Terms Matching

____ 1.	pleasure	A.	noxious stimuli
____ 2.	histamine	B.	synthetic opiate antagonist
____ 3.	C-fibers	C.	opiate primarily in pituitary and brain
____ 4.	enkephalins	D.	analgesia obtained by pressure
____ 5.	endorphins	E.	opiate peptides in cord and adrenal
____ 6.	acupressure	F.	myelinated pain fibers
____ 7.	bradykinin	G.	peptide released by a damaged cell
____ 8.	naloxone	H.	includes "reward"
____ 9.	A-delta fibers	I.	unmyelinated pain fibers
____ 10.	pain	J.	released from mast cells

Short Answer Essay Questions

1. What is stress-induced analgesia? What are its underlying physiological mechanisms?

2. What are enkephalins and endorphins? What are the precursors to these molecules?

3. What are the two regions of the thalamus that contribute to the perception of pain?

4. What is the role of dopamine and the nucleus accumbens in the reinforcing effects of drugs like cocaine and amphetamine?

5. What is Dale's Law? Has it survived intact?

Multiple Choice Questions

1. The substantia nigra contains cell bodies for
   a. norepinephrine
   b. dopamine
   c. serotonin
   d. a & b

2. Local tissue damage causes mast cells to release:
   a. histamine
   b. bradykinin
   c. prostaglandin
   d. serotonin

3. The myelinated fibers that carry nociceptive information into the CNS are the:
   a. C-fibers
   b. substantia gelatinosa
   c. corticothalamic tracts
   d. A-delta fibers

4. A neuroscientific technique where radioactive peptides are used to determine the presence and amount of other peptides is:
   a. autoradiography
   b. thin-layer chromatography
   c. radioimmunoassay
   d. sequence analysis

5. The thalamic area that appears to control the negative affective quality of pain is the:
   a. medial thalamus
   b. spinothalamic tract
   c. lateral thalamus
   d. dorsal thalamus

6. The dorsolateral funiculus is a(n):
   a. ascending analgesia system
   b. ascending hyperalgesia system
   c. descending analgesia system
   d. descending analgeia system

7. Naloxone is a:
   a. synthetic opiate agonist
   b. synthetic opiate antagonist
   c. natural opiate antagonist
   d. type of opiate receptor

8. The enkephalin molecules are:
   a. tripeptides
   b. decapeptides
   c. large proteins
   d. pentapeptides

9. Pro-opiomelanocortin is the precursor molecule to:
   a. leu-enkephalin
   b. met-enkephalin
   c. CRH
   d. endorphin

10. Enkephalins produce analgesia in the spinal cord by:
    a. blocking the release of substance P
    b. blocking opiate receptors
    c. stimluating the release of substance P
    d. stimulating the release of bradykinins

11. A stimulus that an organism will work to obtain is a:
    a. motive
    b. drive
    c. goal
    d. reward

12. The nigrostriatal pathway projects from the:
    a. pons to the caudate
    b. striatum to the substantia nigra
    c. substantia nigra to the striatum
    d. hippocampus to the PAG

13.   Animals self-stimulating their brains in the Olds and Milner paradigm also exhibited various:
   a.   satieted behavior
   b.   appetitive behaviors
   c.   aversive behaviors
   d.   all of the above

14.   The mesolimbic pathway originates in the:
   a.   substantia nigra
   b.   ventral tegmentum
   c.   caudate nucleus
   d.   nucleus accumbens

15.   Cells that are damaged release the peptide:
   a.   bradykinin
   b.   histamine
   c.   substance P
   d.   acetylcholine

Labeling Exercises

1.   Please label this diagram using the terms listed.

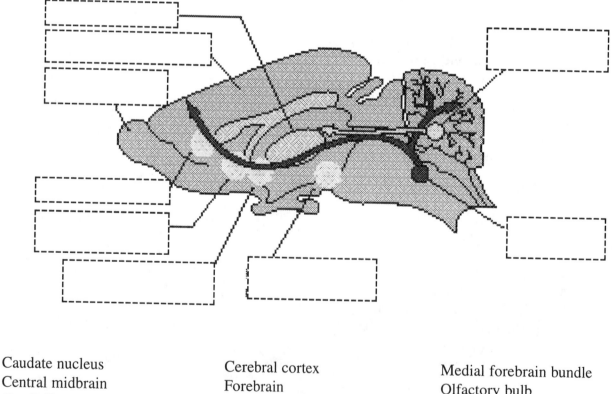

Caudate nucleus   Cerebral cortex   Medial forebrain bundle
Central midbrain   Forebrain   Olfactory bulb
Cerebellar nuclei   Locus coeruleus   Thalamus

2. Please label the diagram using the terms listed.

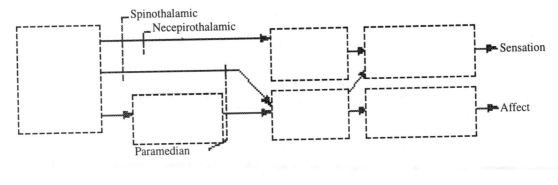

Association Cortex   Medici Thalamus   Somatosensory
Lateral Thalamus   Reticular Formation   Spinal Cord

Answers

Key Terms Matching

1.	H	6.	D
2.	J	7.	G
3.	I	8.	B
4.	E	9.	F
5.	C	10.	A

Short Answer Essay Questions

1. Stress-induced analgesia is the very robust experimental finding that people and animals become analgesic, or less sensitive to pain, when confronted with a wide variety of stressful stimuli. Diverse events such as electric shock, fear, cold water and physical restraint all produce this phenomena. The underlying physiology of stress-induced analgesia is complex. There is clearly an opiate component to it, as evidenced by the fact that opiate antagonists like naloxone block some forms of stress-induced analgesia. However, not all stress-induced analgesia is blocked by opiate antagonists, indicating that there must be a non-opiate component to it as well. There are many candidates for substances that may mediate the non-opiate analgesia, but two strong possibilities are ACTH and cholecystokinin.

2. Enkephalins and endorphins are two classes of endogenous opiate molecules. The enkephalins are pentapeptides that are concentrated in the spinal cord and the adrenal gland. Endorphins are larger molecules than enkephalins and are concentrated in pituitary and brain. The enkephalins are derived from a larger molecule called pro-enkephalin. Pro-enkaphalin produces relatively large quantities of opiate exclusively. The precursor to endorphin, pro-opiomelanocortin (POMC), is cleaved into a number of constituent molecules. As its name implies, POMC is cleaved into endrophin (opio-), melanocyte-stimulating hormone (melano-), and ACTH (cortin).

3. There are at least two thalamic areas that contribute to the perception of pain. The spinothalamic tract interacts with both the medial and lateral regions of the thalamus. The medial thalamus gets a projection from the spinothalamic tract and appears to control the negative emotional quality of pain. Electrical stimulation of the medial thalamus does not produce pain per se, but rather a vague feeling of discomfort which is consistent with its purported role. The lateral thalamus receives a different spinothalamic projection and seems to involve the localization of pain to a particular part of the body. The experience of pain seems to be a combination of activity from these two thalamic nuclei.

4. The dopamine circuit that includes the nucleus accumbens is part of the diffusely projecting mesolimbic pathway. This pathway originates in the ventral tegmentum and projects to a variety of structures. Rats will press a lever thousands of times an hour to receive electrical stimulation of the ventral tegmentum. It appears that the nucleus accumbens is the most

important projection area mediating the reinforcing aspect of this behavior. Dopamine antagonists placed in the nucleus accumbens will make the stimulation to the mesolimbic pathway less rewarding, as the animal will perform significantly less work to get it. Researchers have speculated that it is this natural reward circuit that is activated by addictive compounds such as cocaine and amphetamine. Data have supported this assertion. For example, cocaine injections in the nucleus accumbens increase the amount of extracellular dopamine, and also increases the rewarding nature of electrical stimulation of the ventral tegmentum.

5. Dale's Law, incorrectly attributed to Sir Henry Dale, is the idea that a given neuron only contained one transmitter substance, and used that substance at all of its synapses. Dale's Law is now known to be wrong. A neuron may switch the transmitter it releases during the developmental process. Even a mature neuron may release several transmitter substances. With the flood of information accumulating about peptide molecules being coreleased with classical neurotransmitters, it is clear that Dale's Law is too simple. It may turn out that colocalization of transmitter molecules is not just common, but may in fact be the normal condition for neurons.

Multiple Choice Answers

1.	B	9.	D	
2.	A	10.	A	
3.	D	11.	D	
4.	C	12.	C	
5.	A	13.	B	
6.	C	14.	B	
7.	B	15.	A	
8.	D			

12

Hormones, Sex, and Reproduction

Chapter Summary

This chapter introduces the student to the **endocrine system** and its role in sex and reproduction. All cells synthesize **protein**, and all cells probably use **peptides**, parts of larger proteins, to communicate with other cells. The brain produces peptide hormones via the **pituitary gland**, called the master gland because its products influence the activity of other glands around the body. The pituitary is composed of an **anterior lobe** and a **posterior lobe**. These two regions release numerous hormones that have diverse effects around the body. **Steroid hormones** are a class of hormones, synthesized from **cholesterol**, that don't interact with surface receptors. They produce both **organizational** and **activational** effects on the body and behavior. Steroid hormones produce some of the **sexually dimorphic** characteristics of the adult mammalian brain. They have also been implicated in aggressive behavior. The **estrus** and **menstrual** cycles are also controlled by hormones. The menstrual cycle is divided into a **follicular phase** prior to ovulation and a **luteal phase** after ovulation. Peptide hormones also play a huge role in the maintenance of **pregnancy** and **parturition**. **Pheromones** are essentially external hormones, chemicals that are released from one organism and affect the behavior of another member of the same species. The neural circuitry for mating is complex, given that matign is actually composed of smaller behaviors like **attraction**, **arousal**, and **copulation**.

Chapter Outline

Hormones and "The Master Gland"

      Peptide Hormones

      Peptide Synthesis

Chapter 12   Hormones, Sex, and Reproduction

Learning Objectives

After competing this chapter, you should be able to:

1. Describe how hormones are cleaved from precursor molecules.

2. Discuss the plan of the pituitary gland, and how the two regions are controlled by the hypothalamus.

3. Describe the role of pheromones in behavior.

4. Elucidate the neural circuits for mating and reproduction.

5. Describe the estrus and menstrual cycles.

6. Discuss the idea of critical periods with respect to the development of gender.

Practice Test

Key-Terms Matching

_____ 1. POMC

_____ 2. luetenizing hormone (LH)

_____ 3. testosterone

_____ 4. Wolffian duct

_____ 5. eunuch

_____ 6. paraphilia

_____ 7. vasopressin

_____ 8. Bruce effect

_____ 9. Mullerian duct

_____ 10. somatostatin

A. posterior pituitary hormone

B. female internal genitalia during development

C. causes ovulation

D. inhibits release of growth hormone (GH)

E. castrated man

F. presence of an unfamiliar male terminates a pregnancy

G. mental disorder involving a sexual deviation

H. androgen hormone

I. precursor to ACTH

J. male internal genitalia during development

Short Answer Essay Questions

1. What is POMC? What hormones are produced by the cleaving of this large molecule?

2. What are organization and activational effects of the sex steroid hormones?

3. What are the evolutionary advantages to sexual reproduction over asexual reproduction?

4. What are the phases of the menstrual cycle?

5. What are the effects of steroid hormones on aggressive behavior?

Multiple Choice Questions

1. Females that become synchronized in their estrous cycles after a male appears describes the:
   a. Whitten effect
   b. Vandenbergh effect
   c. Lee-Boot effect
   d. Bruce effect

2. The mammalian homologue to arginine vasotocin (AVT) is:
   a. oxytocin
   b. vasopressin
   c. cortisol
   d. a & b

3. Gametes are :
   a. diploid
   b. haploid
   c. triploid
   d. polychromosomal

4. Thyroxine is produced by the:
   a. anterior pituitary
   b. posterior pituitary
   c. thyroid
   d. spleen

5. Oxytocin and vasopressin are small peptides that each contain only ___ amino acids.
   a. three
   b. five
   c. nine
   d. twenty

6. Lactation is initiated by this hormone:
   a. prolactin
   b. oxytocin
   c. vasopressin
   d. ADH

7. Cortisol is an example of this kind of hormone:
   a. reproductive
   b. glucocorticoid
   c. peptide
   d. none of the above

8. The dexamethasone suppression test is used as a tool to diagnose:
   a. schizophrenia
   b. sexual identity disorders
   c. anxiety
   d. depression

9. The biosynthetic precursor to all the steroid hormones is:
   a. cortisol
   b. thiamine
   c. cholesterol
   d. estradiol

10. Facial hair in males is an example of a:
    a. primary sexual characteristic
    b. secondary sexual characteristic
    c. tertiary sexual characteristic
    d. monomorphic characteristic

11. Building of body mass is called:
    a. anabolism
    b. catabolism
    c. metabolism
    d. parabolism

12. After ovulation, the female is in the _____ of her cycle.
    a. follicular phase
    b. luteal phase
    c. ovular phase
    d. GnRH phase

13.   A chemical signal that can act from one organism to another is a(n):
   a.   hormone
   b.   modulator
   c.   endocrine message
   d.   pheromone

14.   The presence of males accelerates puberty in female mice. This is the:
   a.   Whitten effect
   b.   Vandenbergh effect
   c.   Lee-Boot effect
   d.   Bruce effect

15.   Another name for vasopressin is:
   a.   GnRH
   b.   LH
   c.   ADH
   d.   GH

Labeling Exercises

   1. Please label the diagram using the terms listed.

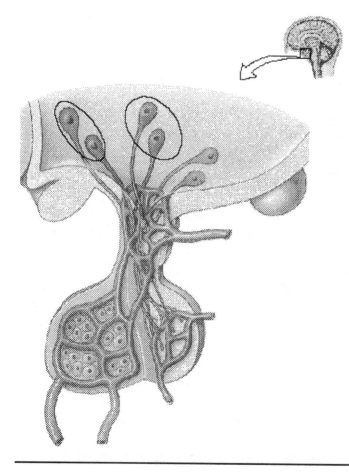

Anterior hypophyseal veins
ANTERIOR PITUITARY GLAND
Capillary beds
Endocrine cells
HYPOTHALAMUS
Inferior hypophyseal artery
Infundibulum
INTERMEDIATE LOBE
Mamillary body
MEDIAN EMINENCE
Optic chiasm
Paraventricular nucleus
Portal veins
Posterior hypophyseal vein
POSTERIOR PITUITARY GLAND
Superior hypophyseal artery
Supraoptic nucleus

2. Please label these diagrams using the terms listed.

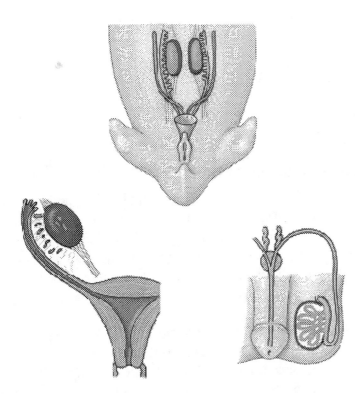

6 week fetus
Female (XX)
Male (XY)

Cortex
Medulla
Mullerian duct
Primordial gonad
Urogenital sinus
With H-Y antigen and TDF
Without H-Y antigen and TDF
Wolffian duct

Fallopian tube
Ovary
Seminal vesicles
Testis
Uterus
Vas deferens

3. Please label these diagrams using the terms listed.

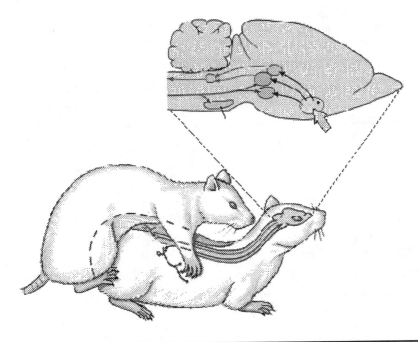

Deep back muscles
High estrogen levels
Lateral geniculate
Lateral vestibulospinal nucleus
Medullary reticular formation
Midbrain reticular formation
MPOA,MAH and VMH
Pressure receptors in flank
Spinal cord

Answers

Key Terms Matching

1. I	6. G
2. C	7. A
3. H	8. F
4. J	9. B
5. E	10. D

1. Pro-opiomelanocortin, or POMC, is a large protein molecule that serves as the precursor to a number of hormones. It is cleaved into smaller pieces by enzymes, and many of the produced segments have biological activity. Perhaps the best known and understood product of POMC is adrenocorticotrophic hormone (ACTH). ACTH is an important mediator of the stress response. Other products include beta-endorphin, met-enkephalin, and several melanocyte-stimulating hormones. These substances all have biological activity of their own, and have also attracted recent research interest because they may interact with ACTH and have some role in the body's response to stress.

2. The sex steroids produce both organizational and activational effects with respect to the determination of gender, as well as other phenomena. Organizational effects are those that occur during the development of the organism, and cause the physical changes that differentiate the genders. The physical changes that are produced also include the development of neural circuits responsible for reproductive behavior. These hormones also produce activational effects, which are those effects that occur throughout the lifespan. The activational effects of steroid hormones are on those structures and circuits that were produced during the organizational phase.

3. There are several distinct evolutionary advantages to sexual reproduction over asexual reproduction. Sexual reproduction first ensures that new genomes can be created from the reassortment of the chromosomes from the parents. Secondly, entirely new chromosomes can be created from the crossing over of genetic material. Third, harmful mutations can be masked in the majority of the offspring by preservation of the normal copy of the gene. In general, sexually reproducing organisms can evolve faster to rapidly changing environmental conditions than asexually reproducing organisms, which produce offspring that are genetically identical to the parent.

4. The menstrual cycle in females is divided conceptually into several phases. A "surge" of GnRH causes the release of estradiol, which produces a further increase in the release of GnRH. The peak of this positive feedback loop culminates in ovulation, and ends the follicular phase of the cycle. After ovulation, the corpus luteum is formed which secretes progesterone into the bloodstream. This part of the cycle is the luteal phase. During this part of the cycle levels of LH, FSH, and estrogen levels fall back to normal. The high levels of progesterone prepare the uterus for a possible pregnancy.

5. The relationship between steroid hormones, particularly androgens, and aggressive behavior is complex. It is clear that males of most species are generally more aggressive than females, and also have higher androgen levels. Male experimental animals that are castrated early in life are also less aggressive then controls, unless supplemented with androgen injections. Finally, human athletes and body builders who take additional steroid hormones for anabolic or performance-enhancing purposes often report increases in aggressive behavior and even violence. However, despite the aforementioned compelling data, correlations between androgen level and aggressiveness tend to be nonexistent. Androgens perhaps play an important role in the development of aggression, but an individual's level of aggression can't be predicted based on an androgen level in the normal range.

Multiple Choice Answers

1.	A	9.	C
2.	D	10.	B
3.	B	11.	A
4.	C	12.	B
5.	C	13.	D
6.	A	14.	B
7.	B	15.	C
8.	D		

Sleep and Dreaming

Chapter Summary

This chapter introduces the student to the topics of sleep and dreaming. Many physiological and behavioral events cycle through a roughly twenty four hour period, and are thus called **circadian rhythms**. The primary neural site that produces these rhythms is a hypothalamic nucleus called the **suprachiasmatic nucleus**. Longer rhythms are primarily caused by the **pineal gland** via the secretion of **melatonin**. Sleep is divided into **non-REM** and **REM** sleep. The various stages of sleep differ from each other physiologically as measured by both the electroencephalogram (**EEG**) and the electromyogram (**EMG**). Non-REM sleep has four discrete stages that have different EEG patterns associated with each. REM sleep is the stage where most dreaming occurs. REM stands for rapid eye movement, which is a characteristic of the stage, as well as the presence of dreams and muscle atonia. There are numerous substances that may function as **sleep-inducing factors**. These include **serotonin, muramyl peptides**, and **adenosine**. There are also substances that appear to function as arousal substances, such as **acetylcholine, norepinephrine**, and **histamine**. Theories of why a need for sleep exists include **immobilization theory** and **energy conservation theory**. Also, the **restorative theory** of sleep postulates that sleep is necessary to repair tissue and restore processes that have been worn down during the waking phase. Finally, the **genetic programming hypothesis** asserts that sleep is necessary to modify innate behavior patterns. **Freud** proposed an influential theory of the purpose of dreams, arguing that they exist to express subconscious motivations of the mind. Finally, there are a number of sleep disorders, including the **insomnias, disorders of rhythmicity, narcolepsy**, and **REM sleep behavior disorder**, and **sleep apnea**.

Chapter Outline

Circadian Rhythms

    About a Day:

        Where is the Clock?

Stages of Sleep

    Different Stages:

        The EEG and EMG

        Non-REM (NREM) Sleep

        Rapid Eye Movement (REM) Sleep

Neural Mechanisms for Sleep and Waking

    The Search for the "Sleep Transmitter"

    Transmitter Systems and "Arousal"

    Box 13-1: The "Reticular Activating System"

    Neural Mechanisms of Dreaming

Why Do We Sleep?

    Box 13-2: Sleep Deprivation Experiments

    Sleep in Evolutionary Perspective

    Restoration or Elimination?

    Jouvet's Theory of Sleep

    Psychological Theories of Dreams

Sleep Disorders

    Insomnias

    Disorders of Rhythmicity

    Other Disorders

    Box 13-3: "Sleeping Medication" and the Elderly

Learning Objectives

After competing this chapter, you should be able to:

1. Describe the EEG and EMG responses during the sleep cycle.

2. Discuss sleep disorders such as insomnia, narcolepsy, night tremors, and REM behavior disorder.

3. Elucidate the various theories about why we sleep.

4. Describe the reticular activating system.

5. Discuss circadian and seasonal rhythms.

6. Describe the theories of why dreaming and REM sleep exist.

Key-Terms Matching

_____ 1. melatonin

_____ 2. Stage 4

_____ 3. awake but drowsy

_____ 4. EEG

_____ 5. sleep spindle

_____ 6. serotonin

_____ 7. K-complex

_____ 8. SCN

_____ 9. EMG

_____ 10. zeitgeber

A. "time giver"

B. internal pacemaker

C. alpha waves

D. measures the electrical activity of the brain

E. measures the electrical activity of muscle

F. high voltage waves

G. produced by pineal gland

H. sleep-inducing monoamine

I. burst of 11-15 Hz waves

J. delta waves

Short Answer Essay Questions

1. Describe the EEG patterns of waking and the various stages of sleep.

2. What are the four groups of insomnias?

3. What are several putative "sleep-inducing" substances in the brain?

4. What are the immobilization and energy conservation theories of sleep? Are there data to support either?

5. What is the activation-synthesis theory of dreaming?

Multiple Choice Questions

1. Melatonin is secreted by the:
    a. SCN
    b. pineal gland
    c. pons
    d. medulla

2. The monoamine implicated in sleep induction is:
    a. norepinephrine
    b. dopamine
    c. adenosine
    d. serotonin

3. The locus coeruleus seems to be important for regulating wakefulness via its projection of:
    a. norepinephrine
    b. serotonin
    c. GABA
    d. epinephrine

4. A compound that may be related to arousal in addition to its role in tissue damage is:
    a. serotonin
    b. GABA
    c. histamine
    d. glycine

5. Dreams with the most substantial plot and sensory experiences occur during:
    a. non-REM sleep
    b. Stage 1 sleep
    c. Stage 4 sleep
    d. REM sleep

6. Dreams are often suppressed by:
   a. MAO inhibitors
   b. tricyclic antidepressants
   c. lithium chloride
   d. SSRI's

7. Approximately 80% of total daily growth hormone release occurs during:
   a. the awake phase
   b. Stage 1 sleep
   c. REM sleep
   d. slow wave sleep

8. According to Freud, the actual contents of a dream are the:
   a. manifest content
   b. dreamwork
   c. latent content
   d. none of the above

9. Uncontrollable attacks of sleep are characteristic of:
   a. night terrors
   b. REM sleep behavior disorder
   c. narcolepsy
   d. insomnia

10. The primary neural site responsible for generating endogenous rhythms is the:
    a. pineal gland
    b. SCN
    c. reticular activating system
    d. pons

11. The transmitter of the retinohypothalamic tract is:
    a. GABA
    b. glycine
    c. arginine
    d. glutamate

12. Caffeine interferes with the activity of this sleep-inducing substance:
    a. adenosine
    b. dopamine
    c. acetylcholine
    d. norepinephrine

13. Seasonal rhythms like hibernation may be regulated by the:
     a. reticular-activating system
     b. SCN
     c. pineal gland
     d. thalamus

14. Somnambulism is most likely to occur in:
     a. REM sleep
     b. Stage 4 sleep
     c. Stage 1 sleep
     d. all stages equally

15. Stage 4 sleep is associated with:
     a. alpha waves
     b. theta waves
     c. beta waves
     d. delta waves

Labeling Exercises

1. Please label this diagram using the terms listed.

Awake, low voltage, random, fast

Drowsy–8 to 12 cps–alpha waves

REM Sleep–low voltage–random, fast with sawtooth waves

Stage 1–3 to 7 cps–theta waves

Stage 2–12 to 14 cps–sleep spindle and K complexes

Stage 4 or Delta Sleep–1/2 to 2 cps–delta waves >75 mV

1 sec

50 mV

K Complexs –

Sawtooth Waves

Sawtooth Waves

Sleep Spindle

Theta Waves

2. Please complete this table using the terms listed.

Table 13-1	FACTORS INVOLVED IN SLEEP AND WAKEFULNESS
Sleep-inducing substances	Arousan-indusing substances

acetylcholine (ACh)
adenosine
delta sleep-inducing peptides (DSIP)
dopamine (DA)
histamine
muramyl peptides (MP) (Factor 5)
norepinephrine (NE)
serotonin

Answers

Key Terms Matching

1.	G	6.	H
2.	J	7.	F
3.	C	8.	B
4.	D	9.	E
5.	I	10.	A

Short Answer Essay Questions

1. The electroencephalogram (EEG) differs markedly between various stages of wakefulness and sleep. An individual who is awake and alert will exhibit beta wave activity, which has the highest frequency of all of the EEG patterns observed. A subject who is awake but drowsy will exhibit more alpha wave activity, which is a moderate frequency wavelength. As the subject falls asleep, a shift towards theta wave activity is observed. Theta waves are even slower frequency waves than alpha and beta, and are characteristic of the lighter stages of sleep. As the subject enters deep sleep, delta waves appear, which are the lowest frequency waves observed. Finally, during the REM stage, the EEG is very active and most closely resembles that of the awake state, although the person is clearly asleep.

2. The insomnias are actually a number of disorders organized into four groups depending on the primary cause. The first group is insomnias that have either behavioral or psychophysiological causes. These insomnias either are a result of excessive worry about falling asleep, or behavioral practices that are deleterious to falling asleep such as stimulant ingestion. The second group of insomnias are those that are secondary to a psychiatric disorder such as depression or schizophrenia. The third group are insomnias that are related to neurological disorders, such as Parkinson's disease. Finally, a group of insomnias exist that are produced by environmental factors such as lighting or temperature. In most but not all cases, treatment of one of the causes or primary conditions will relieve the insomnia.

3. There are a number of putative sleep-inducing factors in the brain. One of the primary ones is serotonin, in particular to the onset of slow-wave sleep. Another one is muramyl peptide, which also produces slow-wave sleep if injected. Another peptide is logically named delta sleep-inducing peptide, because it induces a delta sleep EEG pattern when injected. Finally, adenosine is a nucleotide that may have an inhibitory effect on arousal-inducing transmitters like acetylchline and norepinephrine. The arousing effects of caffeine occur presumably because it has an inhibitory effect on adenosine receptors.

4. The immobilization theory of sleep, associated with Webb, argues that sleep evolved as an adaptive behavior pattern that kept early mammals immobilized and thus safe at night, instead of wandering around being easy prey for nocturnal predators. This theory has a certain appeal, but does not explain why we would still require sleep. The energy conservation

theory argues that sleep exists to conserve energy after food has been gathered. There are some data that support this theory. First, total sleep time and metabolic rate show a very similar developmental pattern. Also, both variables decline with age. Finally, species that have higher metabolic rates tend to sleep more than species with lower metabolic rates.

5. The activation synthesis theory is an attempt to explain the basis of dreaming. Basically, the theory states that dreams are the result of random activation of forebrain structures. The brain interprets the activity as coming from the outside world and the dream is the brain's way of putting together a story from essentially random noise. The theory is consistent with the presence of PGO waves, which are EEG patterns seen during the REM state that would provide the neural stimulation that would produce the dream according to the theory.

Multiple Choice Answers

1.	B	9.	C
2.	D	10.	B
3.	A	11.	D
4.	C	12.	A
5.	D	13.	C
6.	B	14.	B
7.	D	15.	D
8.	A		

14

Eating, Drinking, and Homeostasis

Chapter Summary

This chapter introduces the student to the physiological mechanisms behind eating and drinking, and the concept of **homeostasis**. The brain is the most metabolically active organ in the body. The brain is isolated from the blood circulation by the **blood-brain barrier**. The brain has extensive need for both **glucose** and **oxygen**. These needs require an extensive supply of blood to the brain. New techniques are available to study the metabolic activity of the brain. **Eating**, or feeding behavior, is necessary to supply energy to the body. The physiological systems of the body maintain **homeostasis**, or a stable internal environment. Physiological variables have a **set point**, or optimal level that they will work to maintain. The **glucostatic theory** of hunger states that the level of blood glucose is the critical variable for eating behavior. The **lipostatic theory** argues that eating behavior is regulated by the desire to maintain an ideal weight. Two hypothalamic nuclei have been thought to control hunger and satiety. **The lateral hypothalamus** (LH) is related to hunger and the **ventromedial hypothalamus** (VMH) is related to satiety. Numerous transmitter substances contribute to hunger and feeding. The **monoamines**, especially norepinephrine and serotonin, appear to be particularly important. Also, peptides like **Neuropeptide Y** (NPY) increase appetite. Other peptides like **cholecystokinin** (CCK) appear to be related to satiety. There are a number of **eating disorders**, including **obesity**, **anorexia nervosa**, and **bulimia**. There are a number of physiological mechanisms that are related to thirst and drinking. There are two basic kinds of thirsts, **osmotic thirst** which results from a reduction in water inside cells, and **hypovolemic thirst**, which results from a reduction in water outside cells. Numerous hormones are related to thirst and drinking behavior, including **aldosterone**, **angiotensin I** and **angiotensin II**.

Chapter Outline

Brain Metabolism

    The Brain Needs Energy:

        Blood-Brain Barrier and Glucose Utilization

        Oxygen Requirements

        Circulation Requirements

        Glucose Requirements

Blood Flow

    Perfusion Pressure and Autoregulation

    Blood Supply and Anoxia

Energy Use

    Box 14-1: How Bright Is the Light Bulb?

    Cooling Mechanisms

Techniques for Studying Brain Metabolism

Eating

    Why Do You Eat?

    Homeostasis

    Role of Glucose in Eating Behavior

    Role of lipids in eating behavior

    Hypothalamic Circuits

    Role of Monoamines and Peptide Hormones in Feeding

    Box 14-2: A Role for Insulin in the Brain

    Box 14-3: CCK: A Satiety Hormone?

Eating Disorders

    Breakdowns of Hunger and Satiety Mechanisms:

        Obesity

        Anorexia Nervosa

        Bulimia

Drinking

Why Are You Thirsty?

Thirst

Kidney

Hormonal Modulation: Aldosterone, Vasopressin, and Angiotensin

Learning Objectives

After competing this chapter, you should be able to:

1. Describe the blood flow to the brain.

2. Discuss the subregions of the hypothalamus relevant for hunger and satiety.

3. Elucidate the glucostatic and lipostatic theories of hunger.

4. Describe the two kinds of thirst.

5. Discuss how the body responds physiologically to the two different kinds of thirsts.

6. Describe the concepts of set point and homeostasis.

Practice Test

Key-Terms Matching

_____ 1. osmotic thirst

_____ 2. anoxia

_____ 3. asphyxia

_____ 4. glucagon

_____ 5. set point

_____ 6. CCK

_____ 7. insulin

_____ 8. volemic thirst

_____ 9. homeostasis

_____ 10. hypoglycemia

A. low blood sugar

B. optimal level of activity for a system

C. a "satiety" hormone

D. converts glycogen into glucose

E. converts glucose into to glycogen

F. low blood oxygen

G. complete lack of blood oxygen

H. low water outside cells

I. low water inside cells

J. maintenance of the stability of the internal environment

Short Answer Essay Questions

1. What is the glucostatic theory of hunger?

2. What are the two major kinds of thirst?

3. What are several theories about the physiological cause(s) of obesity?

4. What are two "classic" hypothalamic nuclei that are related to hunger and satiety?

5. What is the hormonal cascade that occurs during volemic thirst?

Multiple Choice Questions

1. The most metabolically active organ in the body is the:
   a. liver
   b. spleen
   c. brain
   d. heart

2. Hyperphagia is a(n):
   a. normal appetite
   b. abnormal increase in thirst
   c. abnormal decrease in appetite
   d. abnormal increase in appetite

3. Electrical stimulation of the ventromedial hypothalamus (VMH) causes a(n):
   a. decrease in food intake
   b. decrease in fluid intake
   c. increase in food intake
   d. increase in fluid intake

4. Neuropeptide Y (NPY) appears to increase appetite by interacting with this peptide:
   a. VIP
   b. galanin
   c. CCK
   d. vasopressin

5. An eating disorder characterized most saliently by severe self-starving is:
   a. obesity
   b. Krone's disease
   c. anorexia nervosa
   d. bulimia

6. Blood loss will produce:
   a. osmotic thirst
   b. intracellular thirst
   c. volemic thirst
   d. none of the above

7. Osmoreceptors are located in cells of the:
   a. VMH
   b. glomerulus
   c. subfornical organ
   d. preoptic nucleus

8. A hormone secreted by the kidneys which causes us to retain sodium is:
   a. aldosterone
   b. renin
   c. angiotensin
   d. vasopressin

9. Angiotensin II stimulates receptors in the:
   a. kidneys
   b. preoptic area
   c. subfornical organ
   d. supraoptic nucleus

10. Aldosterone stimulates a salt appetite via its effects on the:
    a. preoptic area
    b. medial amygdala
    c. OVLT
    d. subfornical organ

11. Although only 2-3% of the total weight of the body, the brain consumes about _____ of the total oxygen.
    a. 5%
    b. 10%
    c. 20%
    d. 30%

12. The difference between the arterial blood pressure and the cerebral venous pressure is the:
    a. perfusion pressure
    b. mean arterial pressure
    c. metabolic pressure
    d. glycolytic pressure

13. The carotid arteries merge with the basilar artery to give rise to the:
    a. preoptic nucleus
    b. OVLT
    c. cerebral portal vessel
    d. circle of Willis

14. The origin of the term homeostasis is attributed to:
    a. Bernard
    b. Cannon
    c. Jouvet
    d. Selye

15. Bilateral lesions of the lateral hypothalamus (LH) produces:
    a. decreases in fluid intake
    b. decreases in food intake
    c. increases in food intake
    d. increases in fluid intake

Labeling Exercises

1. Please label these diagrams using the terms listed.

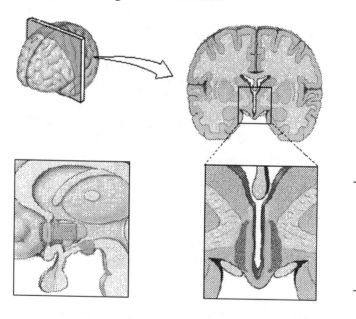

Hypothalamus	Mammillary body	Periventricular
Lateral	Medial	Periventricular nucleus
Lateral nuclei	Medial nuclei	Third ventricle

2. Please label the diagram using the terms listed.

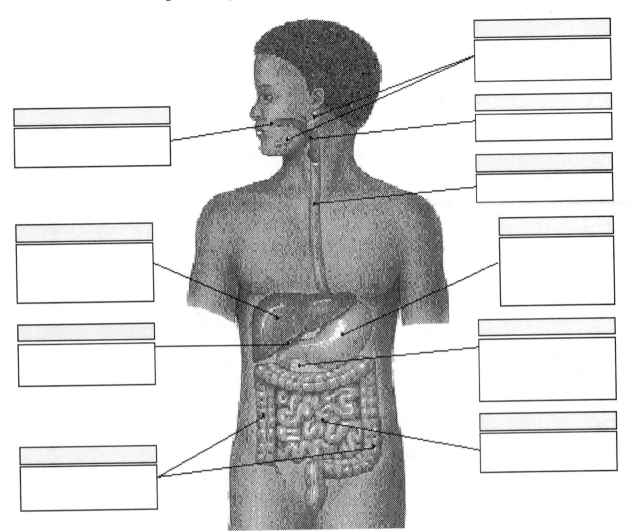

ESOPHAGUS

GALLBLADDER

LARGE INTESTINE

LIVER

ORAL CAVITY, TEETH,
   TONGUE

PANCREAS

PHARYNX

SALIVARY GLANDS

SMALL INTESTINE

STOMACH

Chemical breakdown of materials via acid and enzymes; mechanical processing through muscular contractions

Dehydration and compaction of indigestible materials in preparation for elimination

Enzymatic digestion and absorption of water, organic substrates, vitamins, and ions

Exocrine cells secrete buffers and digestive enzymes into small intestine; endocrine cells secrete hormones into the blood

Mechanical processing, moistening, mixing with salivary secretions

Pharyngeal muscles propel materials into the esophagus

Secretion of bile (important for lipid digestion), storage of nutrients, many other vital functions

Secretion of lubricating fluid containing enzymes that break down carbohydrates

Storage, concentration, and release of bile for fat emulsification

Transport of materials to the stomach

Answers

Key Terms Matching

1.	I	6.	C
2.	G	7.	E
3.	F	8.	H
4.	D	9.	J
5.	B	10.	A

Short Answer Essay Questions

1. The glucostatic theory of hunger states that the key variable in producing hunger and eating behavior is the level of blood glucose. The theory runs into problems with diabetes, however, a condition characterized by extremely high blood glucose levels due to a deficiency in insulin. According to glucostatic theory, diabetics should not be hungry, given their high levels of blood glucose. However, diabetics tend to show a hyperphagia. Apparently it is not the amount of glucose in the blood that is important, but rather inside cells. There are receptors sensitive to glucose level both in the liver and the lateral hypothalamus. Low levels of glucose in cells, as detected by these receptors, leads to feeding behavior.

2. There are two major kinds of thirst, osmotic thirst and hypovolemic thirst. Osmotic thirst results from a decrease in water from the intracellular compartment. This could happen from an increase in salt ions extracellularly, for example. Water will then diffuse from inside cells to balance the concentrations, and osmotic thirst will ensue. Hypovolemic thirst results from a decrease in fluid from the extracellular compartment. A loss of blood, for example, will result in a loss of both water and salt from the extracellular environment, which both must be replaced.

3. There are numerous theories about the phyiological causes of obesity. One theory asserts that obese individuals are genetically or environmentally prone to high levels of insulin. Fat therefore is stored rather than available for energy use. Organisms therefore have plenty of calories, but they are not available for use, and this causes the person to seek more. This theory suggests that obesity for some people may be essentially a metabolic disorder involving the insulin system. Obese people may also have a different hypothalamic homoestatic set point than normal weight controls. Finally, there are some data to suggest that obese individuals may produce more endogenous opioid peptides than normal weight controls. This notion is corroborated by animal research that demonstrates that genetically obese rats have elevated endorphin levels.

4. The two hypothalamic nuclei with a classic role in hunger and satiety are the lateral (LH) and ventromedial (VMH) hypothalamus. Classic lesion and stimulation data appeared to show that the LH was the "hunger center" of the brain and the VMH was the "satiety center". Although these two structures are clearly related to hunger and satiety, it is now clear

that the early characterization was oversimplified. LH lesions, for example, causes the release of free fatty acids from stores and this probably causes the dramatic reduction in feeding that is observed. VMH lesions, by contrast, cause increases in gastric emptying and insulin levels which may be primary factors in the dramatic hyperphagia that is observed.

5. Volemic thirst produces a complex hormonal cascade to retain water and salt, and to motivate the organism to get more of each. The kidneys respond to low blood volume by secreting the hormone renin. Renin causes the conversion of angiotensin I to angiotensin II in the bloodstream. Angiotensin II produces numerous effects throughout the body. First, it causes the release of aldosterone from the kidneys, which acts to retain salt and increase salt appetite. Second, it causes the release of vasopressin (antidiuretic hormone) from the the pituitary, which causes the organism to retain fluid. Finally, angiotensin II stimulates the subfornical organ which may initiate drinking behavior via a connection to the median preoptic area.

Multiple Choice Answers

1.	C	9.	C
2.	D	10.	B
3.	A	11.	C
4.	B	12.	A
5.	C	13.	D
6.	C	14.	B
7.	D	15.	B
8.	A		

Development and Learning

Chapter Summary

This chapter introduces the student to the topics of development and learning. The nervous system starts out from the **ectoderm**, or outer layer of the developing organism. A **neural plate** of cells forms, which eventually comes together to form the **neural tube**. Throughout the course of development neuronal **proliferation** occurs, neurons must **migrate** to their final destinations, and they become **differentiated** from other cell types. The tips of developing axons, called **growth cones**, are guided by **tropic factors**. They are also nourished by **trophic factors** like **nerve growth factor** (NGF). **Synaptogenesis** is the formation of synapses after developing axons have reached their targets. **Learning** is the inference we make about a change in behavior. Learning is presumably mediated by changes in the nervous system, a general process called **neural plasticity**. **Nonassociative learning**, such as **habituation** and **sensitization**, is learning without the formation of an association between stimuli or events. **Associative learning** does entail the formation of associations between stimuli or events. **Classical conditioning** is the formation of an association between two stimuli, whereas **operant conditioning** is the formation of an association between a behavior an an environmental event. The study of simple organisms can enable neuroscientists to potentially understand the cellular changes that accompany learning. The study of the **gill-withdrawal reflex** in *Aplysia*, for example, has demonstrated that habituation is due to decreased neurotransmitter release by the sensory neuron. The **hippocampus** seems to be the critical structure responsible for encoding **declarative memories**. The hippocampus, as well as other brain structures, exhibit **long-term potentiation** (LTP), an increase in synaptic strength following brief, high frequency stimulation. LTP is mediated by **NMDA** glutamate receptors.

Chapter 15   Development and Learning

Chapter Outline

Development of the Nervous System

Neurogenesis

      Making Neurons:

            Embryonic Development and Induction

            Cell Proliferation

Neuronal Migration

Neuronal Differentiation

      Neuronal Fate Determination

      Determination of Neurotransmitter Phenotype

      Development of Electrical Properties

Axon Development and Growth Cone Guidance

      Tropic Factors and Other Guides

      Box 15-1: Levi-Montalcini and Nerve Growth Factor

      Adhesion Molecules

      Molecular Gradients

Synaptogenesis

      The Development of Synapses

Activity-Dependent Fine-Tuning of the Nervous System

      Box 15-2: The Visual System as a Model for Development and Plasticity

Learning Theory

      Nonassociative Learning: Habituation and Sensitization

      Associative Learning

      Complex Learning

      Box 15-3: Learning of Birds Song: A Novel Neural Mechanism

Learning Objectives

After competing this chapter, you should be able to:

1. Describe neurogenesis, migration, and differentiation of developing neurons.

2. Discuss the process of synapse formation, including the role of trophic factors and competition.

3. Differentiate between associative and nonassociative learning and define habituation, sensitization, and classical conditioning, and operant conditioning.

4. Describe the studies with *Aplysia* that examine the synaptic changes that occur during habituation, sensitization, and conditioning.

5. Describe both the cellular basis of, as well as the perceived importance of LTP.

6. Discuss the studies looking at the physiological changes that occur during the nicitating membrane response.

Practice Test

Key-Terms Matching

_____ 1. imprinting

_____ 2. operant conditioning

_____ 3. habituation

_____ 4. ectoderm

_____ 5. mesoderm

_____ 6. classical conditioning

_____ 7. mitosis

_____ 8. spatial learning

_____ 9. endoderm

_____ 10. sensitization

A. progressively weaker response to a repeated stimulus

B. learning to navigate through one's environment

C. increased response to a repeated weak stimulus

D. association between a behavior and an environmental event

E. inner layer

F. outer layer

G. cell proliferation

H. forming a strong attachment to the first significant stimulus seen after birth

I. association between two stimuli

J. middle layer

Short Answer Essay Questions

1. What synaptic changes occur in *Aplysia* during habituation?

2. How do tropic and trophic factors contribute to developing neurons?

3. What are imprinting and critical periods?

4. What is LTP? Why does it appear to fit a model of memory formation in the brain?

5. Describe nervous system development from fertilization of the egg up to the development of specific brain divisions.

Multiple Choice Questions

1. Another term for the "forebrain vesicle" is the:
    a. ventricular layer
    b. mesencephalon
    c. marginal layer
    d. prosencephalon

2. The tip of a newly extended axon is called the:
    a. target zone
    b. growth cone
    c. integrin
    d. trophic area

3. Directional cues for developing axons are provided by:
    a. adhesion molecules
    b. trophic factors
    c. filopodia
    d. basal laminae

4. Progressively weaker responses to a repeated stimulus is:
    a. habituation
    b. dishabituation
    c. sensitization
    d. associative learning

5. Salivation to food describes a(n):
    a. conditioned stimulus
    b. conditioned response
    c. unconditioned stimulus
    d. unconditioned response

6. An animal incorporates nonspecific information about an environment that appears to facilitate later learning of specific things in that environment. This describes:
    a. imitative learning
    b. spatial learning
    c. latent learning
    d. observational learning

7. Studies of *Aplysia* demonstrate that during habituation:
    a. the sensory neuron releases less transmitter after the same action potential
    b. the sensory neuron fires less action potentials
    c. the motor neuron downregulates its receptors
    d. the sensory neuron fires more action potentials

8.   The search for the engram, the putative physical basis of a memory, is most associated with:
   a. Pavlov
   b. Kandel
   c. Hebb
   d. Lashley

9.   The process of transforming short-term memories into long-term memories is called:
   a. retrieval
   b. consolidation
   c. acquisition
   d. storage

10.   The neural plate folds over onto itself, forming the:
   a. blastocyst
   b. endoderm
   c. neural tube
   d. neural crest

11.   The inability to remember events subsequent to an injury to the brain is:
   a. retroactive amnesia
   b. retrograde amnesia
   c. anterograde amnesia
   d. dissociative amnesia

12.   The structure that appears most critical for the formation of declarative memories is the:
   a. hippocampus
   b. hypothalamus
   c. pons
   d. basal ganglia

13.   The critical receptor mediating long-term potentiation (LTP) is:
   a. GABAA
   b. GABAB
   c. D_2
   d. NMDA

14.   The receptor in the previous question is for the transmitter:
   a. glycine
   b. glutamate
   c. GABA
   d. serotonin

15. The nicitating membrane response has been extensively studied in:
 a. rats
 b. *Aplysia*
 c. *Hermissenda*
 d. rabbits

Labeling Exercises

1. Please label this diagram using the labels listed.

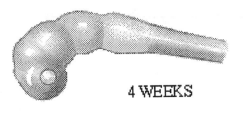

4 WEEKS

Diencephalon
Mesencephalon
Metencephalon
Myelencephalon
Telencephalon

2. Please label this diagram using the labels listed.

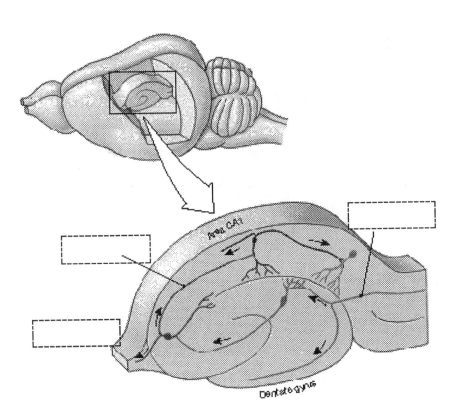

Area CA3

Perforant pathway

Schaeffer collateral fiber pathway

3.   Please label this diagram using the labels listed.

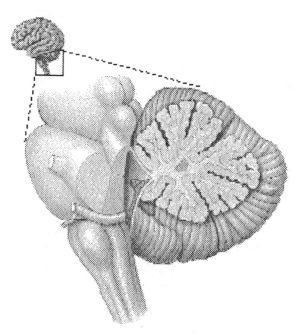

Anterior lobe
Arbor vitae
Cerebellar cortex
Cerebellar peduncles
Choroid plexus of the fourth ventricle
Dentate interpositus nucleus
Flocculonodular lobe
Inferior
Medulla oblongata
Middle
Pons
Posterior lobe
Superior

Answers

Key Terms Matching

1.	H	6.	I
2.	D	7.	G
3.	A	8.	B
4.	F	9.	E
5.	J	10.	C

Short Answer Essay Questions

1. The synaptic changes that occur during habituation in *Aplysia* have been extensively studied. There are sensory neurons that receive information from the mantle and siphon, which cover the gill. These neurons synapse directly onto motor neurons that mediate the gill-withdrawal reflex if a stimulus is received by the sensory neurons. Repeated presentations of a stimulus to the mantle results in habituation of the gill-withdrawal response. Research from Kandel's lab demonstrated that the habituation of the response is due to a presynaptic change. The sensory neurons continue to produce action potentials in response to a perturbation of the mantle, but release less transmitter to the same action potential.

2. Developing neurons are assisted by both tropic and trophic factors. Tropic factors provide directional cues for developing neurons through a variety of mechanisms. They are chemicals that can both repel or attract developing neurons to an appropriate target. Trophic factors are other substances that typically don't provide directional cues for axons, but rather support their growth. The best understood trophic factor is nerve growth factor (NGF), although NGF also has tropic function as well.

3. Imprinting is a complex form of classical conditioning observed in some animals. Many species form a strong attachment to the first stimulus that they see after birth. Typically, the stimulus would be their mother, so the adaptive value of the response is clear. This response enhances the survival chances of the young because the mother provides nourishment and protection. Imprinting was extensively studied by the ethologist Konrad Lorenz. Lorenz substituted himself for the mother of newly hatched ducklings. The ducklings imprinted on him, and followed him as they would their mother. Other research indicated that some species will imprint on objects that are even inanimate. Finally, imprinting only occurs during a limited time after birth, called the critical period.

4. Long-term potentiation (LTP) is a change in the strength of a synapse that is possibly a mechanism for the formation of memory. It was discovered in the early 1970s in the hippocampus, and has been demonstrated in many other regions subsequently. The initial discovery was recording from dentate gyrus neurons, after stimulating afferent perforant path cells. After high frequency stimulation to the perforant path, the dentate cells show exaggerated responses to weak test stimuli. The response to the weak test stimuli was therefore

potentiated. The excitement over LTP is due to the fact that the response matches our conception of what memory formation may look like on a neural level. Presumably, synapses would be strengthened during learning and memory, and LTP appears to be a model of synaptic strengthening.

5.   The development of the nervous system begins very soon after conception in the human embryo. The fertilized egg first develops into many cells, called blastomeres, around a central cavity or blastocoel. The entire structure at this point is called the blastocyst. During the subsequent gastrulation phase, the blastomeres migrate and form three layers, the ectoderm, mesoderm, and endoderm. The ectoderm is the layer that gives rise to the nervous system. The next stage, neurulation, involves ectodermal cells forming a neural plate, which then folds over itself to become the neural tube. It is the neural tube that will become the brain and spinal cord. During the formation of the neural tube, some cells break away to form the neural crest, which becomes autonomic and spinal ganglia. Finally, cell specialization begins, along the neural tube, which become the future distinct divisions of the brain.

Multiple Choice Answers

1.	D	9.	B
2.	B	10.	C
3.	B	11.	C
4.	A	12.	A
5.	D	13.	D
6.	C	14.	B
7.	A	15.	D
8.	D		

16

Language and Higher Cognitive Function

Chapter Summary

This chapter introduces the student to the concepts of language and higher cognitive function. The study of human **neurobiology** has many theoretical limitations to it. Much information has been deduced regarding brain function from **diagnostic neurology**, the localization of brain damage based on behavioral impairments. There are a number of classic neurological deficits observed after various kinds of brain damage. **Aphasias** are difficulties with speech. **Broca's aphasia** is a deficit in speech production whereas **Wernicke's aphasia** is a deficit in speech comprehension. **Apraxia** is the inability to move without cognitive intent. **Agnosias** are problems with knowing parts of one's own body. **Dyslexias** are problems with reading ability. The experience of **emotion** is mediated by many structures that are subcortical. The **hippocampal formation** appears to be a critical structure for the formation of long-term declarative memories. There are a number of **organic brain syndromes**, that are not the result of damage or trauma. **Down syndrome** is a chromosomal disorder characterized by facial abnormalities and problems with brain development. **Phenylketonuria** results from an inability to metabolize phenylalanine and is characterized by mental retardation. **Cerebellar ataxia** can result from repeated blows to the head, and is often seen in boxers. **Korsakoff's disease** is often seen in chronic alcoholics, and **Alzheimer's disease** is seen in many elderly individuals. Many new imaging techniques, such as **PET**, **MRI**, and **CAT**, are available that enable neuroscientists to see the activity of the brain. Finally, much of our information about the function of the brain has been gleaned from studies stimulating different brain regions in an awake patient.

Chapter Outline

Human Neurobiology

      Theoretical Limits and Practical Problems

      Box 16-1: The Importance of Introspection

Results from Communication in and with Other Species

Results from Diagnostic Neurology

      Aphasias

      Apraxias

      Agnosias

      Box 16-2: Prosopagnosia and "Blindsight"

      Alexias

      Dyslexia

      Box 16-3: Lateralization of function

      The Concepts of Latent Circuits and Latent Function

      Emotion

      Memory

Organic Brain Syndromes

      Down Syndrome

      Phenylketonuria

      Cerebellar Ataxia

      Korsakoff's Disease

      Spongiform Encephalopathies

      Alzheimer's Disease

Epilepsy

Results from Noninvasive Imaging Techniques

    Positron Emission Tomography (PET)

    Magnetic Resonance Imaging (MRI)

    Computerized Axial Tomography (CAT)

    Cerebral Blood Flow Measurements

    Electrical and Magnetic Records Across the Skull

Results from Brain Stimulation

    Neurosurgery on Awake Individuals

    Penfield's Observations

Consciousness and the Self

    Is it Possible to be "Less of a Person"?

    Box 16-4: Unilateral Neglect

Learning Objectives

After competing this chapter, you should be able to:

1. Discuss the theoretical limits and practical problems of human neurobiology.

2. Describe how diagnostic neurology has contributed to our knowledge of brain function.

3. Discuss how emotions and memories are processed by the brain.

4. Elucidate the characteristics of organic brain syndromes like Down syndrome, Parkinson's, Phenylketonuria, and Korsakoff's.

5. Describe how new noninvasive technologies have contributed to our knowledge of brain function.

6. Discuss how Penfield's stimulation studies led to an increased understanding of brain function.

Practice Test

Key-Terms Matching

_____ 1. Broca's aphasia

_____ 2. prosody

_____ 3. alexia

_____ 4. implicit memory

_____ 5. Down syndrome

_____ 6. explicit memory

_____ 7. microcephaly

_____ 8. syntax

_____ 9. Wernicke's aphasia

_____ 10. agraphia

A. deficit in speech comprehension

B. inability to read

C. conscious recollection

D. the rhythm and melody of speech

E. small head size

F. difficulty in producing speech

G. the ordering of word into meaningful statements

H. trisomy 21

I. inability to write

J. unconscious and unintentional

Short Answer Essay Questions

1. Describe Broca's and Wernicke's area. What does damage to each produce?

2. What is Down syndrome?

3. What is cerebellar ataxia and why is it so common in boxers?

4. What is prosopagnosia?

5. What is diagnostic neurology and how did it acquire most of its information?

Multiple Choice Questions

1. Phenylketonuria is a genetic disease where infants have abnormally high levels of _____ in their urine.
    a. tryptophan
    b. tyrosine
    c. phenylalanine
    d. glucose

2. Usually the first brain region affected in a victim of pugilistic dementia is the:
   a. cerebellum
   b. pons
   c. hippocampus
   d. thalamus

3. Korsakoff's disease is directly caused by a dietary deficiency of:
   a. thiamine
   b. phenylalanine
   c. tyrosine
   d. tryptophan

4. Accumulation of beta-amyloid plaques are diagnostic of:
   a. spongiform encephalopathy
   b. Alzheimer's disease
   c. epilepsy
   d. cerebellar ataxia

5. A deficit in comprehension of speech but retention of speech fluency describes:
   a. global aphasia
   b. Broca's aphasia
   c. prosody
   d. Wernicke's aphasia

6. The inability to move is:
   a. agnosia
   b. aphasia
   c. agraphia
   d. apraxia

7. A patient suffering from prosopagnosia is unable to:
   a. speak in whole sentences
   b. remember names
   c. remember faces
   d. encode new memories

8. "Lateralization of function" means:
   a. right-handed people are more spatial than left-handed people
   b. function is segregated between the cerebral hemispheres
   c. aggregate field theory
   d. "higher" organisms have larger cranial capacities

9. The brain area thought to be most responsible for the expression of emotion is the:
    a. limbic system
    b. pons
    c. cerebellum
    d. arcuate fasciculus

10. Damage to this cortical area can produce humorless moralism, religiosity, and obsessive-ness:
    a. frontal lobe
    b. thalamus
    c. parietal lobe
    d. temporal lobe

11. Explicit is to implicit as:
    a. unconscious recall is to conscious recall
    b. conscious recall is to unconscious recall
    c. unconscious recall is to classical conditioning
    d. classical conditioning is to unconscious recall

12. The particular limbic structure damaged in Korsakoff's patients that impairs their memories is the:
    a. thalamus
    b. hypothalamus
    c. mammillary bodies
    d. hippocampus

13. If Penfield stimulated a section of motor cortex, the result was:
    a. involuntary contralateral movement
    b. voluntary contralateral movement
    c. voluntary ipsilateral movement
    d. ipsilateral somatosensation

14. Estimates are that language developed no earlier than:
    a. 10,000 years ago
    b. 500,00 years ago
    c. 1,000,000 years ago
    d. 100,000 years ago

15. The rhythm, inflection, timbre, and melody of speech is:
    a. prosody
    b. grammar
    c. syntax
    d. phasia

Labeling Exercises

1. Please label the diagram using the terms listed.

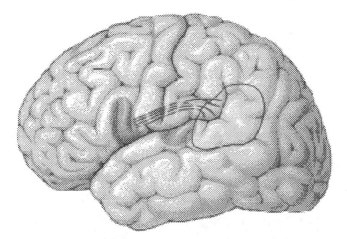

Arcuate fasciculus

Auditory cortex

Broca's area

Prefrontal cortex

Wernicke's area

2. Please label the diagram using the terms listed.

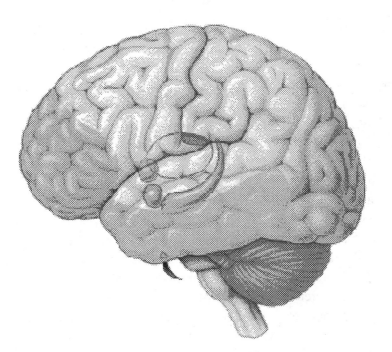

Amygdala	Inferotemporal cortex
Basal forebrain	Mediodorsal nucleus of thalamus
Cerebellum	Prefrontal cortex
Hippocampus	Rhinal cortex (on meidal surface of temporal lobe)

Answers

Key Terms Matching

1.	F	6.	C
2.	D	7.	E
3.	B	8.	G
4.	J	9.	A
5.	H	10.	I

Short Answer Essay Questions

1. Broca's area is part of motor association cortex in the frontal lobe. Wernicke's area is part of association temporal cortex. Both are left hemisphere structures, and are part of a language circuit that includes the arcuate fasciculus. Discrete damage to each produces unique behavioral deficits involving language. Damage to Broca's area produces Broca's aphasia, a disorder involving speech production. Speech is labored, word-finding difficulty (anomia) is typical, and mispronunciations and poor grammar are common. Little deficits are seen with the comprehension of spoken or written words. Damage to Wernicke's area causes Wernicke's aphasia, a difficulty in the comprehension of speech. These patients can produce speech, although it is usually incomprehensible, but does not comprehend speech.

2. Down syndrome, or Trisomy 21, is a chromosomal disorder involving the production of an extra 21st chromosome. The disorder is characterized by the development of a very small brain, distinctive facial abnormalities, temporal lobe difficulties, and a developmental disability that is not treatable. There are also commonly heart defects and chronic sinus problems. Down syndrome becomes increasingly common as the age of the mother increases. Technology is available now to screen for this condition and inform the parents. Finally, there is a tremendous range of abnormalities and mental deficiencies in Down individuals.

3. Cerebellar ataxia is an irreversible form of damage to the cerebellum that is primarily a disorder of movement, although other deficiencies may occur. Movement is characterized by an unsteady gait, hand tremors, and disturbances in speech and thought processes. Cerebellar ataxia is one form of pugilistic dementia, a very common disorder among boxers. The cerebellum is particularly vulnerable to damage after a blow to the head because of its physical location in the brain. Since is is in the very back of the brain, a sharp blow to the head will cause the cerebellum to hit the back of the skull and become damaged. Another reason for the cerebellum's vulnerability is the tremendous number and density of its neurons. Since these neurons are very active, they have high metabolic requirements and often are the first cells damaged if the person suffers metabolic stress.

4. Prosopagnosia is a disorder characterized by the inability to recognize faces. It results from damage to the right hemisphere of the temporal and occipital lobes. Prosopagnosia can vary in severity, ranging from nonrecognition of few or some faces up to the lack of the concept

of what a face even is. Some patients are unaware that they even have a deficit, because the memory of faces is apparently stored in the same location as the recognition mechanism. Given the incredible number of faces that one encounters, encodes, and remembers throughout the lifespan, it is not surprising that there is a complex neural mechanism to support that ability.

5. Diagnostic neurology is the deduction of the location of a brain injury based on the behavioral impairments observed. This systematic pairing of behavioral problems with later identification of the site of the injury greatly enhanced our knowledge of the brain, and localization of function. Different brain regions are not equally susceptible to injury, however. Basal ganglia structures, for example, are particularly prone to vascular damage and thus much information was acquired about their function. Brainstem structures, however, where damage is typically lethal, remained somewhat of a mystery. Diagnostic neurology acquired much information about the function of the brain during times of war, when a tremendous number of injuries to the brain occurred.

Multiple Choice Answers

1.	C	9.	A
2.	A	10.	D
3.	A	11.	B
4.	B	12.	C
5.	D	13.	A
6.	D	14.	D
7.	C	15.	A
8.	B		

17

Psychopharmacology

Chapter Summary

This chapter introduces the student to the actions of drugs on the brain and behavior. Drugs can be grossly divided into **agonists** and **antagonists**. Agonists mimic or facilitate the action of an endogenous transmitter. Antagonists block the activity of an endogenous transmitter. Drugs must be **administered** via one of several routes, they become **distributed** around the body, and they must be **eliminated** by the body. **Tolerance** is the effect of needing more and more drug to achieve the same effect. **Addiction** is the psychological and physiological need for a drug, and **withdrawal** is the syndrome produced by the abrupt cessation of taking a drug. The **Opponent Process Theory** explains many drug phenomena by the body attempting to maintain homeostasis. CNS **depressants** produce a general decrease in behavior and cognition. **Alcohol** and **marijuana** are two commonly used CNS depressants. Both produce effects by interacting with receptor systems in the brain. **Barbiturates** are a class of depressants formerly used as sedatives. Their medical role has been taken by the **benzodiazapines,** a class of compounds that includes **valium** and **librium**. These drugs facilitate transmission at **GABA** receptors and thus increase inhibition in the brain. The CNS **stimulants** are drugs that increase behavior and cognition. Two common legal stimulants are **caffeine** and **nicotine**. Two common illegal ones are **amphetamine** and **cocaine**. These compounds produce their effects by blocking reuptake of the **catecholamines**. **Hallucinogens** are compounds whose primary effect is to induce hallucinations, and includes **mescaline**, **MDMA**, and **LSD**. Finally, **opiates** are drugs like **morphine** and **heroin** that produce analgesic and euphoric effects by interacting with **opiate receptors** in brain.

Chapter Outline

Agonists and Antagonists

Pharmacokinetics

    Administration

    Distribution

    Elimination

Addiction, Tolerance, and Withdrawal

    Opponent Process Theory

Central Nervous System Depressants

    Slowing the CNS:

        Alcohol and Marijuana

        Mechanism of Action: Membrane Theories

        Mechanism of Action: Receptor Theories

        Sedatives and Tranquilizers

        Mechanism of Action: The Prospect of Natural Ligands

        Box 17-1: The GABA Receptor Complex

        Mechanism of Action: Chloride Conductance and CNS Output

Central Nervous System Stimulants

    Speeding Up the CNS:

        Nicotine and Caffeine

        Amphetamines and Cocaine

        Mechanism of Action: Dopamine autoreceptors

        Mechanism of Action: Dopamine reuptake

        Box 17-2: The Problem of Specificity

Hallucinogens

    Mechanism of Action: Results of Neuropharmacology

Opiates

    Mechanism of Action: Heterogeneity of Opiate Receptors

    Mechanism of Action: Natural Opiate Agonists and Synthetic Opiate Antagonists

Learning Objectives

After competing this chapter, you should be able to:

1. Describe pharmacokinetics, including administration, distribution, and elimination of drugs.

2. Discuss the opponent process theory and how it applies to drug tolerance, addiction, and withdrawal.

3. Describe how the various CNS depressants produce their effects within the CNS.

4. Describe the role of dopamine in the reinforcing effects of amphetamine and cocaine.

5. Discuss the effects of the hallucinogenic compounds, and the ideas about their mechanism of action.

6. Describe the subclasses of opiate receptors in brain, and what effects are associated with each.

Practice Test

Key-Terms Matching

_____ 1. agonist

_____ 2. tolerance

_____ 3. metabolites

_____ 4. THC

_____ 5. librium

_____ 6. anxiolytic

_____ 7. anxiogenic

_____ 8. addiction

_____ 9. antagonist

_____ 10. half-life

A. drug that prevents activity of endogenous transmitter

B. amount of time it takes to eliminate half of a drug dose from the body

C. the physiological and psychological need for a drug

D. drug that mimics or facilitates the action of the endogenous transmitter

E. anxiety-producing

F. first benzodiazapine marketed

G. anxiety-reducing

H. more and more drug is required for a desired effect

I. psychoactive ingredient in marijuana

J. component molecules of a drug

Chapter 17 Psychopharmacology

Short Answer Essay Questions

1. What is Opponent Process Theory? How does it explain phenomena like tolerance, addiction, and withdrawal?

2. What are the various routes of drug administration in humans? What are the pluses and minuses of each?

3. What are the mechanisms of action whereby ethanol causes its numerous effects?

4. What are the mechanisms of action of amphetamine and cocaine?

5. What are the effects of LSD?

Multiple Choice Questions

1. In humans, the most common route of drug administration is:
   a. oral
   b. intravenous
   c. intraperitoneal
   d. intramuscular

2. The blood-brain barrier is an obstacle for:
   a. hydrophobic compounds
   b. all compounds
   c. hydrophilic compounds
   d. ethanol

3. According to Opponent Process Theory, the automatic effects a drug produces is the:
   a. A-process
   b. B-process
   c. (A-B)
   d. none of the above

4. Ethanol is metabolized by the enzyme:
   a. acetaldehyde
   b. alcohol dehydrogenase
   c. thiamine
   d. disulfiram

5. Ethanol influences the activity of the:
   a. GABA receptor
   b. NMDA receptor
   c. glycine receptor
   d. a & b

6. Anandamide is:
   a. an opiate receptor antagonist
   b. a treatment for alcoholism
   c. the endogenous compound that utilizes the THC receptor
   d. an exogenous substance that activates 5-HT2 receptors

7. The first benzodiazapine marketed, in 1960, was:
   a. xanax
   b. valium
   c. librium
   d. trazadone

8. An inverse agonist at the benzodiazapine receptor would be:
   a. anxiogenic
   b. anxiolytic
   c. anxiety-reducing
   d. a & b

9. Nicotine is an agonist at a receptor subtype for:
   a. dopamine
   b. norepinephrine
   c. acetylcholine
   d. GABA

10. The reinforcing effects of amphetamine and cocaine are presumably due to their increasing activity of:
    a. norepinephrine
    b. dopamine
    c. GABA
    d. acetylcholine

11. The fastest route of drug administration is:
    a. oral
    b. intravenous (i.v.)
    c. intraperitoneal (i.p.)
    d. intramuscular (i.m.)

12. The active ingredient in peyote is:
    a. LSD
    b. MDMA
    c. PCP
    d. mescaline

13. An effect of opiate drugs is:
    a. analgesia
    b. dysphoria
    c. hyperalgesia
    d. none of the above

14. Most drugs are metabolized by the:
    a. kidney
    b. nephrons
    c. liver
    d. stomach

15. The GABA receptor that interacts with depressant drugs surrounds a channel for this ion:
    a. Cl-
    b. Na+
    c. K+
    d. Ca++

Labeling Exercise

1. Please label this diagram using the terms listed.

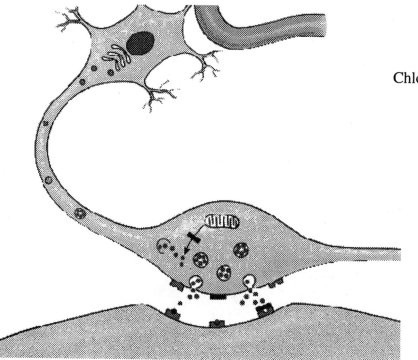

Amphetamine
Apomorphine
Capillary
Chlorpromazine Haloperidol
Cocaine
Dopamine
Dopamine autoreceptor
Pargyline
Postsynaptic receptor
Reserpine
Vesicular dopamine

2. Please label this diagram using the terms listed.

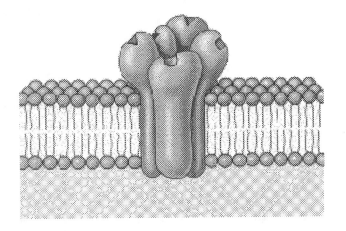

Barbiturate site

Benzodiazapine site

GABA site

Answers

Key Terms Matching

1. D
2. H
3. J
4. I
5. F

6. G
7. E
8. C
9. A
10. B

Short Answer Essay Questions

1. Opponent Process Theory is an excellent explanation of many of the effects of drugs. The critical assumption is homeostasis. Opponent process theory argues that a stimulus like a drug causes a series of changes in the body collectively called the "A process". Once an A process has been initiated, it's opposite, the "B process", is automatically produced to maintain homeostasis. Repeated exposure to stimuli like drugs build up the B process, and don't change the A process, thus the person experiences tolerance. If the A process is pleasurable, then the B process must be painful, so addiction can be defined as continued drug use to avoid the painful B process. Finally, removal of the drug will also remove the A process, and only leave the painful B process, producing the painful symptoms of withdrawal.

2. There are a number of routes of injection for introducing drugs into the body. The most common route in humans is oral, with the obvious advantage of convenience. However, the drug must be able to survive the harsh environment of the stomach for some period of time to be effective. The oral route is also relatively slow, and is thus not the best choice in an emergency situation. A second method is intravenously (i.v.). The major advantage of the i.v. method is speed, since the drug goes directly into the bloodstream. A major drawback is the high concentrations of drug reached very quickly, and thus the potential for overdose. More rarely used methods include subcutaneous, intramuscular, and rectal routes. All of these three routes are relatively slow. Finally, drugs can be directly inhaled by the lungs, which also produces very high blood levels very quickly.

3. Ethanol has several physiological effects in the brain which make it a CNS stimulant. First, ethanol induces a "membrane fluidization" effect at all neuronal membranes in the CNS. In the presence of ethanol, cell membranes become more flexible than normal, and this disrupts all membrane-related processes. Second, although there is no specific ethanol receptor in brain, ethanol appears to affect to receptor systems. Ethanol potentiates GABA activity at its inhibitory receptor, and thus increases inhibition in the brain. Finally, ethanol also appears to inhibit activity at the NMDA glutamate receptor. Alcohol therefore potentiates the activity of a major inhibitory transmitter and impairs the activity of a major excitatory transmitter.

4.   The CNS stimulants, amphetamine and cocaine, share similar mechanisms of action that explain their similar effects. Both compounds block the reuptake of the catecholamines, norepinephrine and dopamine. This action would potentiate the activity of any catecholamine released. Although blocking the reuptake of norepinephrine will produce effects, it is commonly accepted that increasing dopamine activity is related to the highly pleasurable experience of these compounds, and thus their severe abuse potential. Amphetamine also increases catecholamine release, which is one of the reasons it has longer lasting effects than cocaine.

5.   Lysergic acid diethylamide (LSD) produces a variety of effects upon ingestion. There are some mild peripheral effects that include increases in heart rate and blood pressure, and dilation of the pupils. These effects are mild, as compared to the primary effects regarding perceptual alterations. LSD causes serious alterations in sensory distortions, thought disruptions, and hallucinations. Less common effects include psychotic episodes and synesthesia, a mixing of sensory modalities. An individual experiencing a synesthesia event will report "seeing language" or "hearing colors."

Multiple Choice Answers

1.	A	9.	C
2.	C	10.	B
3.	A	11.	B
4.	B	12.	D
5.	D	13.	A
6.	C	14.	C
7.	C	15.	A
8.	A		

The Biology of Mental Illness

Chapter Summary

This chapter introduces the student to the biology of mental disorders. Mental disorders are described and categorized in the **Diagnostic and Statistical Manual** (DSM IV). The **medical model** assumes that all mental disorders have a biological origin. The **schizophrenias** are a group of disorders characterized by disordered communication, perception, and thought. Schizophrenics show **florid symptoms** like paranoia and delusions, but may also show **negative symtoms** such as isolation and catatonia. The first drug introduced to treat schizophrenia, called a neuroleptic, was **chlorpromazine**. Since all neuroleptics bind to dopamine receptors, the **dopaminergic hypothesis** of schizophrenia argues that schizophrenia may be an excess of dopamine neurotransmission in some parts of the brain. Neuroleptics typically have a side effect of **tardive dyskenesia**, which resembles Parkinson's symptoms and is a result of dopamine blockade in motor centers. Recently, it has been postulated that schizophrenia has a **viral etiology**, given that the incidence rate increases if the mother experiences influenza during the second trimester. **Affective disorders** are disorders where the primary symptom is affect or mood disturbances. **Mania** is a form of affective disorder characterized by accelerated thought, grandiose ambitions, and increases physical and sexual appetites. **Depression** is conceptually the opposite of mania, including **suicidal ideation, anhedonia,** and **psychomotor retardation**. Individuals with **bipolar illness** cycle between episodes of mania and depression. Individuals with **Seasonal Affective Disorder** (SAD) become depressed during the winter. A number of antidepressant medications have been developed including **MAO inhibitors, tricyclics,** and **SSRI's**. **Anxiety disorders** are characterized by excessive fear and avoidance behavior, and are typically treated with benzodiazapine drugs.

Chapter Outline

Learning Objectives

After competing this chapter, you should be able to:

1. Compare and contrast the antipsychiatry movement with the medical model of mental illness.

2. Describe the dopaminergic hypothesis of schizophrenia.

3. Describe the symptoms of unipolar depression, mania, and bipolar disorder.

4. Discuss the various antidepressant medications, including their mechanism of action and side effects.

5. Describe the anxiety disorders and their treatment.

6. List some of the philosophical and physical problems associated with psychotrophic medications.

Practice Test

Key-Terms Matching

_____ 1. Thomas Szasz

_____ 2. Pargyline

_____ 3. Chlorpromazine

_____ 4. tardive dyskinesia

_____ 5. Imipramine

_____ 6. delusions of grandeur

_____ 7. catatonia

_____ 8. Ugo Cerletti

_____ 9. Prozac

_____ 10. John Cade

A. discoverer of electroconvulsive shock

B. SSRI

C. negative symptom

D. tricyclic

E. MAO inhibitor

F. discoverer of lithium

G. side effect of neuroleptics

H. first neuroleptic

I. antipsychiatry movement

J. florid symptom

Short Answer Essay Questions

1. What is the dopaminergic hypothesis of schizophrenia? List several pieces of evidence to support it.

2. What is seasonal affective disorder and how is it treated?

3. What are some of the side effects of the MAO inhibitors?

4. What are some serious drawbacks to the use of many psychotropic medications?

5. What is or was the antipsychiatry movement? How has it changed in recent years?

Multiple Choice Questions

1. The first neuroleptic drug introduced was:
   a. chlorpromazine
   b. clozapine
   c. sertraline
   d. pargyline

2. Neuroleptics all have the common mechanism of being:
   a. dopamine agonists
   b. norepinephrine antagonists
   c. dopamine antagonists
   d. norepinephrine agonists

3. The dopamine projection that regulates the release of pituitary peptides is the:
   a. nigrostriatal projection
   b. tuberoinfundibular projection
   c. mesolimbic system
   d. none of the above

4. Tardive dyskinesia often results from:
   a. short-term depressant administration
   b. short-term benzodiazapine administration
   c. paranoid schizophrenia
   d. long-term neuroleptic administration

5. The type of schizophrenia characterized by an increase in receptors of the D2 type is:
   a. Type I
   b. Type II
   c. Type III
   d. iatrogenic

6. The fear of public places is:
   a. catatonia
   b. agoraphobia
   c. claustrophobia
   d. sociophobia

7. Unipolar illness is:
   a. equally likely in men and women
   b. twice as likely in men as in women
   c. twice as likely in women as in men
   d. virtually unknown in men

8. A characteristic of mania is:
   a. accelerated thought processes
   b. illusions of invincibility
   c. exaggerated sexual appetite
   d. all of the above

9. Melatonin, an indoleamine, is secreted by the:
   a. pituitary
   b. pineal
   c. hypothalamus
   d. thyroid

10. MAO inhibitors were largely abandoned as antidepressants because a serious side effect was:
    a. hypertension
    b. psychotic episodes
    c. low blood sugar
    d. mania

11. Prozac is one of the atypical antidepressants that are relatively specific for:
    a. serotonin
    b. norepinephrine
    c. GABA
    d. dopamine

12. A proponent of the antipsychiatry movement was:
    a. Bleuler
    b. Freud
    c. Szasz
    d. Kraeplin

13.   Catatonia is an example of a:
      a.   florid symptom of schizophrenia
      b.   synesthesia
      c.   relapse
      d.   negative symptom

14.   An iatrogenic condition is one that is:
      a.   genetic in origin
      b.   caused by a doctor
      c.   based on a biological predisposition
      d.   none of the above

15.   The lack of pleasure in food, sex, etc., is:
      a.   hedonia
      b.   anhedonia
      c.   catatonia
      d.   psychomotor retardation

Labeling Exercises

1.   Please complete this table using the terms listed on the next page.

Table 18-1	PROPOSED DIVISION OF SCHIZOPHRENIA INTO TWO CATEGORIES BASED ON SYMPTOM VARIETY	
	Type I	Type II
Symptoms		
Response to neuroeptics		
Intellectual impairment		
Dyskinasia		
Underlying pathological changes		
Eponym		

(a) D$_2$ receptors increased

(b) VIP in amygdala increased

Absent

Absent

Bleuler

Cell loss in temporal lobe including cells of parahippocampal gyrus and CCK nd somatostain cells in hippocampus

Good

Negative (esp. poverty of speech)

Pinel and Haslam

Poor

Positive

Present

Sometimes present

2.   Please label this diagram using the terms listed.

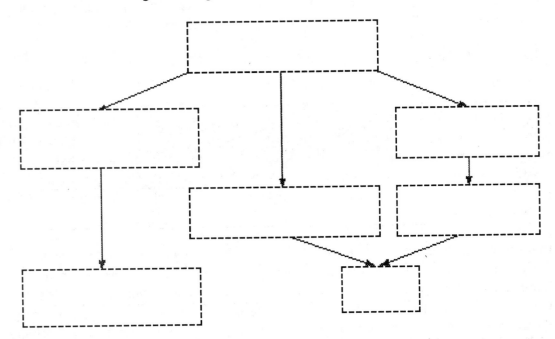

Ambiguous unstructured sensory input

Delusional beliefs

Heightened awareness of irrelevant stimuli

Intrusion of unexpected/unintended material from long-term memory

Perception not influenced by memory

Preference for, and reduced symptoms in, highly structured, predictable environments

Answers

Key Terms Matching

1.	I	6.	J
2.	E	7.	C
3.	H	8.	A
4.	G	9.	B
5.	D	10.	F

Short Answer Essay Questions

1. The dopaminergic hypothesis of schizophrenia is the notion that schizophrenia is an excess of dopamine in some regions of the brain. There are several good pieces of data to support this hypothesis. First, all neuroleptic drugs bind to dopamine receptors and are antagonists there. In fact, there is a positive correlation between binding affinity and clinical efficacy. There are also data which show that schizophrenics have higher levels of brain dopamine than normal controls. This is measured post-mortem. The development of atypical neuroleptics which have less of an effect on dopamine systems may simply underscore the fact that a schizophrenic diagnosis may reflect a number of different underlying biological problems.

2. Seasonal affective disorder, with the apt acronym SAD, is the experience of depression in the winter as the days become shorter and the nights become longer. The sufferer will sleep late in the morning, have little or no energy, and often gain weight due to increased appetite and food intake. SAD appears to be a disorder of rhymicity. A promising treatment is using strong artificial light to mimic sunlight. Dietary supplements of melatonin have also been used, but are probably ineffective. SAD seems clearly to be a disorder of rhythms, and fits well with observations of other depressed patients who also exhibit disturbances of bodily rhythms.

3. Inhibitors of monoamine oxidase (MAO) were the first class of antidepressants developed. These drugs inhibit MAO, which is a synaptic enzyme that breaks down the monoamine transmitters. These drugs would presumably have the effect of increasing monoaminergic transmission, at least in the short term. A major problem with these drugs is the presence of catecholamines in the autonomic nervous system. These drugs can alleviate depression, but can also lead to dangerous or lethal peripheral side effects like hypertension and increased heart rate. It was mostly these side effects which led to the development of other antidepressant drugs.

4. The psychotrophic medications as a group, although having an enormous effect on society and medicine, are not without serious problems. First, many of the drugs were discovered serendipitously, and how they work is poorly understood, meaning that many problems may exist. Many of the compounds may also have addictive potential, leaving the patient with

an additional medical problem from the one that initially required treatment. Some drugs may increase the risk of suicide, partly because of their delay in therapeutic efficacy. Finally, many have side effects that are debatably as serious as the original disorder for which the drug was prescribed.

5. The antipsychiatry movement, associated with individuals such as Thomas Szasz and R. D. Lang, arose in the 1960s and 1970s. The basic tenant of the movement, opposed to the medical model, was that all psychiatric illness, no matter how serious, was the result of social trauma. The appropriate treatment, therefore, was not medication but interventions like group therapy. Many seriously ill patients were released as a consequence of this movement, often to disastrous consequences. Although a number of individuals oppose the extensive use of medications currently, the obvious benefits of psychotropics and the apparent biological basis of many psychiatric disorders make the antipsychiatry approach seem dated.

Multiple Choice Answers

1.	A		9.	B
2.	C		10.	A
3.	B		11.	A
4.	D		12.	C
5.	A		13.	D
6.	B		14.	B
7.	C		15.	B
8.	D			